Praise for *A Nose for Trouble*

"Anyone who knows Michael Ainslie—as I do—is better for the experience. Anyone who reads Michael's fascinating story will be better for the experience as well. *A Nose for Trouble* is a smart testament to a life well lived."

—**James Patterson**, best-selling author

"Michael Ainslie has led many different lives—all well lived. He has been an entrepreneur, a CEO, a board member, a consultant, and a mentor to countless people. These roles have involved him with both commercial enterprises and with not-for-profit organizations. He has led this fast-paced life hardly pausing for breath between assignments. The reader will share Michael's exciting career and marvel at how much he has accomplished."

—**Ron Daniel**, Managing Partner Emeritus, McKinsey & Company

"Very few people have lived a life that so reflects the touchstones that have defined our country in the last half century to now: in fine art, real estate, and finance. An insider on all fronts, Michael Ainslie's story is the stuff of high adventure—rarely lived and more rarely told."

—Joni Evans; Co-founder, wowOwow.com and PureWow.com; former Publisher, Simon and Schuster; former Publisher, Random House; former Vice President and Senior Literary Agent, the William Morris Agency

"Michael captures the grit and heart of mission-driven leadership in this revealing book that demonstrates the power of vulnerability, authenticity and courage when organizational change is imperative."

—Shirley M. Collado, PhD; President, Ithaca College; Posse 1, Vanderbilt University Class of 1994

"A fascinating story of talent and motivation leading to wildly successful achievement of the American Dream, this is a brilliant insider's tour of a life lived deeply and woven of the threads of some of the great institutions of America. *A Nose for Trouble* is told through the eyes of an engaging, generous, and loving man who has a gift for sustaining lifelong relationships and whose great joy is building deep and productive connections between people that often pay off in unexpected ways."

—Peter T. Scardino, former Chief of Surgery, Memorial Sloan Kettering Cancer Center

A NOSE
FOR
TROUBLE

SOTHEBY'S, LEHMAN BROTHERS,
AND MY LIFE OF REDEFINING ADVERSITY

MICHAEL AINSLIE

with **RICHARD EVANS**

GREENLEAF
BOOK GROUP PRESS

This book is a memoir reflecting the author's present recollections of experiences over time. Its story and its words are the author's alone. Some details and characteristics may be changed, some events may be compressed, and some dialogue may be recreated.

Published by Greenleaf Book Group Press
Austin, Texas
www.gbgpress.com

Distributed by Greenleaf Book Group

For ordering information or special discounts for bulk purchases, please contact Greenleaf Book Group at PO Box 91869, Austin, TX 78709, 512.891.6100.

Design and composition by Greenleaf Book Group and Kim Lance
Cover design by Greenleaf Book Group and Kim Lance
Cover photograph: ©2019 FredoLego via iStock / Getty Images Plus Collection

Photos of Michael Ainslie with Barbara Bush; with Nancy Reagan and Alan Boyd; and at the "Save the Capitol" rally: To the extent the National Trust for Historic Preservation holds copyright to these photographs or a license to use and distribute them, the National Trust grants to Greenleaf Book Group a nonexclusive royalty free perpetual license to publish the images in works authored by Michael Ainslie.

Photo of Michael Ainslie with Baron Hans Heinrich Thyssen-Bornemisza and Henry Ford II: To the extent that Warren Mattox (Mattox Photography) owns the rights to this photograph, Mattox Photography grants permission for its use in this book.

Publisher's Cataloging-in-Publication data is available.

Print ISBN: 978-1-62634-671-0

eBook ISBN: 978-1-62634-672-0

Part of the Tree Neutral® program, which offsets the number of trees consumed in the production and printing of this book by taking proactive steps, such as planting trees in direct proportion to the number of trees used: www.treeneutral.com

TreeNeutral

Printed in the United States of America on acid-free paper

19 20 21 22 23 24   10 9 8 7 6 5 4 3 2 1

First Edition

To my wife, Suzanne—my partner and best friend. She has centered me for thirty-three years. Her love and wise counsel have been vital to my ability to cope with a long list of difficult personalities and to laugh with and enjoy the many wonderful folks along the way.

Contents

Introduction

'VE ALWAYS BEEN THE KIND of person who looks for things I can change. Instead of being attracted to established, well-oiled organizations, I seek out ways to tackle problems and lead in new directions. I approach things not as they are but as they might be with a different vision. Maybe it's because I get bored easily. Maybe it's because I embrace adventure. But only rarely have I made the mistake of taking on a job that did not require some kind of fixing. I've always looked for a challenge, something complicated, something entrepreneurial, and frequently, that has led to trouble.

As I reflect on my experiences, I'm aware that virtually every decade of my life has led me to some degree of trouble. I originally thought I would be sharing a tale of change and leadership with you, but when a good friend told me I seem to always have had a "nose for trouble," I realized my stories of change and leadership exist, in large part, because of the troubles I've encountered along the way. In fact, some of the greatest lessons of my life and best things I have to offer are a direct result of the adversities I've faced.

In my teens, a rare autoimmune disease almost killed me. In my early twenties, during the Cold War, I narrowly avoided arrest by a Russian soldier in the frozen wasteland of the Finnish-Soviet border. Later that same year, I was the sole passenger on a small Air America plane that lost an engine over a Vietcong-occupied jungle, the pilot needing to make an emergency landing in an active war zone. In my thirties, the oil embargo of 1973–74 doomed my first real business venture, a luxury resort in Puerto Rico, requiring I do some fancy footwork to stave off bankruptcy for my company and search for a new way to provide for my family of six.

In my late fifties, at the end of a successful ten years as CEO of Sotheby's, I became enmeshed in one of the most public price-fixing scandals of the twentieth century. Though I played no part in it and wasn't guilty of wrongdoing, simply having my name linked to the company and its travails spelled trouble in that period of my life.

In my midfifties and early sixties, I was on the board of Lehman Brothers. I was one of the ten people in the boardroom who cast a vote on the night that Lehman was forced to declare bankruptcy. Afterward, in the wake of the 2008 financial crisis, I was asked to become chairman of the Lehman estate, working hard for the next four years to salvage what was left of the bankrupt company.

Though, thankfully, the past decade of my life has been relatively trouble-free, what has become obvious to me over the years is that I have a high tolerance for risk, and that can lead to multiple outcomes. In spite of the troubles I've encountered and trials I've endured, there have been some very good outcomes too: The Posse Foundation, in its infancy and a big risk when I became its first board chair, has turned out to be one of the greatest success stories in American higher education over the past three decades. My alma mater, Vanderbilt University, has risen to become one of America's highest-rated universities, and I had fun helping to steer that growth during my twenty-one years on its board of trustees. The United States Tennis Association, facing many problems when I joined its board in the late '90s, has enjoyed remarkable growth over the years, partly through initiatives I helped lead. I've also had the great honor and privilege of using what I've learned and earned throughout my life to participate in acts of philanthropy for good causes.

In the end, this *is* a memoir about change and leadership but also about what it looks like to learn and grow in the face of adversity, move forward in spite of troubles, and discover you have more to offer the world. I don't believe adversity has to knock you down. Even if it causes you to stumble, you can learn from it, be strengthened by it, and ultimately be better *because* of it. I've seen firsthand that a person can succeed and rise due to highly ethical behavior and a willingness to do the right thing. While any one of my own difficult moments in life could have stopped me in my tracks, I chose to move forward, not to be defeated. This story, my life story, is about how to make the best out of trouble and how to redefine your misfortunes, and I write it for you, in hopes that it will inform your story too.

Lehman Brothers— September 14, 2008

1

The Vote in the Boardroom

I **T WAS A FLEETING MOMENT,** a few minutes in time, when we, as the board of Lehman Brothers—nine men and one woman sitting in the large paneled boardroom at the company headquarters on West Fifty-Second Street late on the Sunday evening of September 14, 2008—flirted with the perhaps irresponsible idea of refusing to face reality: refusing to buckle to the demands of the federal government and the Securities and Exchange Commission (SEC). We considered refusing to vote to send this 158-year-old company into bankruptcy.

Had we done so, the financial storm that hit the world economy when the stock markets opened a few hours later in Asia would have turned into a tsunami and created even more havoc. Had we done so, Lehman Brothers, one of the major global investment houses, would not have been the only firm unable to meet its financial obligations, and the shock would have sent markets plummeting at an even faster rate than they did in the next few days.

But the moment passed, and we knew we had to do what was necessary to minimize the oncoming chaos.

Our board consisted of Dick Fuld, the chairman and CEO of Lehman, who, over the previous decade, had guided us to the heights we'd achieved; seven other former CEOs (including me); Henry Kaufman, a leading economist; and Marsha Evans, a retired US Navy admiral. We were not irrational people, and after a long discussion, which helped control some of the fear and resentment we were all feeling, we understood we would need to confront the inevitable.

Lehman Brothers, although the smallest of the four major investment banking houses, had recently been the most successful of the four, riding high on the wave of prosperity that ran through the American economy in the early years of the twenty-first century. But that was before the subprime catastrophe ruined everything.

Lehman Brothers was involved in subprime, of course, but not nearly to the same extent as Merrill Lynch, which was in the process of being bought by Bank of America. Given our predicament, we had wanted the protection of a partner too, and then Barclays Bank showed interest in coming to our aid with a buyout offer. During fourteen intense telephonic board meetings that were held in the days preceding our vote—before we were each ordered to get on a plane for New York to deal with the "pending crisis"—there had been much discussion about the Barclays bid, with a general acceptance that it was the only way to go. But we'd learned that according to British law, any major takeover was required to be put to the vote of *all* Barclays shareholders, a number that presumably ran into the hundreds of thousands. Due to the seriousness of the situation and potential global impact, we'd requested and thought we might be granted a waiver of this requirement, but it became clear in the final days that the waiver was not forthcoming. According to Treasury Secretary Henry Paulson, the Chancellor of the Exchequer, Alistair Darling, refused to grant the waiver, saying the United Kingdom did not want to "import your cancer."[1] He did not seem to be aware that "Lehman's UK subsidiary, LBIE, was financed entirely by the parent. Thus the September 15 bankruptcy filing triggered LBIE's bankruptcy, immediately importing the Lehman event to Britain. It was naïve for the CFO of the United Kingdom to not comprehend the global nature of Lehman and any other large financial institution."[2]

In the final discussions before our vote, we were left to contemplate the barely believable scenario of our great company going bankrupt as the Federal Reserve deserted us, Barclays was unable to execute its plan to merge with Lehman, and JPMorgan Chase, our own clearing bank, was helping itself to Lehman's money.[3]

Jamie Dimon, the CEO of JPMorgan Chase, and his management team held meetings with Secretary Paulson and Chairman Ben Bernanke on Tuesday, September 9. While the content of their discussions is not known, it is most interesting to note that immediately following those meetings, Steve Black, head of JPMorgan's investment bank, called Dick Fuld and demanded overnight changes in Lehman's guaranty and security agreements and $5 billion in new cash as collateral in order for Lehman to reopen the next day. In that final week before the bankruptcy, JPMorgan Chase shored up against its Lehman exposure by demanding and receiving from Lehman $8.6 billion in increased cash and near cash collateral. While the New York District Court later upheld JPMorgan Chase's right to make these demands, clearly they were a major contributing factor to Lehman's loss of liquidity in the final days. "JPMorgan Chase & Co (JPM.N) will pay $1.42 billion in cash to resolve most of a lawsuit accusing it of draining Lehman Brothers Holdings Inc of critical liquidity in the final days before that investment bank's September 2008 collapse," read a January 25, 2016 *Reuters* piece. According to the same article, the settlement "resolves the bulk of an $8.6 billion lawsuit accusing JPMorgan of exploiting its leverage as Lehman's main 'clearing' bank to siphon billions of dollars of collateral just before Lehman went bankrupt on Sept. 15, 2008, triggering a global financial crisis. Lehman's creditors charged that JPMorgan did not need the collateral and extracted a windfall at their expense."[4]

Given this scenario, it was hardly surprising that evening that we so seriously considered refusing to do what we were being asked to do. Yet in the domed ceiling of the oak-paneled boardroom where we met, a disembodied voice spoke through a speaker, asking us to do the unavoidable. The man speaking to us was Christopher Cox, head of the SEC, and rather than directing his words to Dick Fuld on this evening, he'd chosen to address us all as a board. Although I did not see Cox as a strong head of the SEC, at that moment his voice carried all the weight he needed, and it spelled doom for Lehman Brothers.

Reacting to what we were being told, Tom Cruikshank, a director who was formerly CEO of Halliburton, asked angrily, "Is the federal government directing us to put Lehman into bankruptcy?"

And in a phrase he seemed to enjoy, Cox answered, "You need to do what you need to do." By this, he meant that we needed to vote to bankrupt Lehman Brothers. We asked Cox, who was hemming and hawing around, to put the general counsel of the Federal Reserve Bank of New York, Thomas Baxter, on the phone, and only after Baxter made it clear that the government would not provide any financing did we know the jig was really up. Sadly, we realized we had no choice but to bankrupt Lehman Brothers.

We voted the way we did after it became clear that the government was not going to help us out. It was the largest bankruptcy in world history, and I am still convinced it was unnecessary. Allowing Lehman to become a bank holding company would have solved the crisis for the moment; the federal government, however, continued to refuse to approve this request and provide the financing needed to keep Lehman alive. In spite of this refusal, one week after the bankruptcy, the government granted bank holding status to Goldman Sachs, Morgan Stanley, and Merrill Lynch. A week earlier on September 7, 2008, the Treasury had been authorized to buy $100 billion of Freddie Mac and Fannie Mae preferred stock and securities.[5] In the days following Lehman's bankruptcy, they provided $85 billion in financing to save AIG.[6] Still to this day, it is unclear why Lehman was singled out and not allowed to access government financing.

Few people had a view into what we as a board knew on that evening of September 14. But I was in the room, I understood that there was more— far more—behind the sequence of events, and I believe there are individuals who, to this day, never accepted responsibility for bringing about a calamity that hurt so many people in the aftermath.

Personally, I experienced a deep range of emotions that evening—anger that Lehman had been singled out as the fall guy, while other firms were surviving through takeovers; exasperation that the mistakes that had been made had led to that outcome; and a flickering moment of fear when I realized that what happened in that room would impact people I knew and loved.

With a sinking heart, I watched bright young people carrying cardboard boxes full of their belongings out of the Lehman building that night. It was news that shocked the world, and they left under the intense glare of television klieg lights. I remember walking wearily back to my apartment at midnight, the full enormity of the situation before me.

In the end, while my personal predicament was nothing compared to that of so many others, I was floored by how things had transpired. I needed all the love I could get, and thankfully, I got plenty from my daughter Serena, who was ten at the time; my older children; and my incredible wife, Suzanne. At one point, as they watched news of the debacle on television, Serena turned to her mother and said, "It's okay, Mommy. I can sell all my toys on eBay." When I heard this, all I could do was smile in gratitude at her sweetness and resolve.

I knew we'd be able to move forward, and, in all honesty, financial woes were the least of my worries. After the vote in the Lehman boardroom, I sought answers for the unnecessary bankruptcy that played a role in the global financial crisis that followed for several years. I wanted to shed light on the truth so we could do things differently next time, learn from the experience, be wiser. I reflected on who I was, what I brought to the table, and how I could leverage my experiences—even from something as terrible as this—to lead to a better outcome for the next crisis. Though this was a hard moment in my personal and professional history, I knew I'd faced adversity before and I could do something about it. I could write my future, as I'd done during other times of trouble in my life.

Early Years

2

Early Lessons in Life

NEVER HAD THE CHANCE TO meet my paternal grandfather, George Ainslie, but I understood him to be a bug scientist who studied beetles, among other insects,[1] and he'd done so with such academic attention to detail and research that one can find online pictures of what became known as the Ainslie eye beetle. Born in 1887, he lived in Tennessee and taught at the University of Tennessee in Knoxville as a professor of entomology. He worked for the Department of Agriculture and became an expert in his field before dying, somewhat mysteriously, in 1932 at the young age of forty-five. The family thought it was stomach cancer, but in those days, causes of death were frequently not understood.

My grandfather's early death left my father, George Lewis Ainslie, who was then sixteen years old, as the male head of the family with the prospect of supporting his mother and his sister. It became clear he could not afford the luxury of a college education, and he set about devising ways of creating some income. One of them involved raising chicks in the basement of his family's Knoxville home, which worked fine until he nearly squashed my grandmother one day when she, a petite lady, was in the basement, inspecting the hatchery; the big six-foot-tall incubator that warmed the tiny chicks came crashing down on her one-hundred-pound frame, but with my father's help, she managed to escape with nothing more than a few bruises.

In those days, my father delivered papers and swept the floors at the local branch of National Cash Register (NCR), a company founded in 1884 in Dayton, Ohio, by John H. Patterson. Patterson, whose company would likely have become the IBM of the postwar years had he not made the mistake of firing the young executive who later went on to create IBM,[2] developed the cash register for businesses to keep track of sales. The cash register, eventually fully transistorized as a business computer and named the NCR 304, was in those days a mechanical machine made up of thousands of parts and pieces. My father proved quite adept at taking these machines apart and reassembling them—often in our garage. The people at NCR in Knoxville quickly recognized my father's skills with his hands and liking for things mechanical and sent him off to the company headquarters in Dayton, Ohio, for training.

During this time, he met my mother, Jean Claire Waddell, at the First Baptist Church in Dayton. They were married in August 1939, a month before the outbreak of World War II in Europe. As a very young couple— Dad was twenty-three and Mom only nineteen—they faced an uncertain future. But, by this time, Dad was a certified NCR repairman, and he was sent to work in Johnson City, Tennessee, one of the Tri-Cities, located in the northeast corner of Tennessee. About this time, he received a 4-F rating from the US Army, granting him a medical exemption from military service due to his flat feet, and thus he did not get called up for WWII.

The family grew, with my sister, Ellen, arriving first in 1941, then me, born in 1943, followed by my brother Peter in 1946, and finally my youngest brother, David, born in 1950. That year, when I was seven, my father was appointed service manager in NCR's Bristol branch. Only twenty-five miles from Johnson City, Bristol was another of the Tri-Cities. It was there that I developed my love of sports. I became a very good pitcher in Little League, fell in love with basketball, and later took up track, competing in the high jump and 440-yard dash.

Five years later, we made a move to the third of the Tri-Cities, Kingsport, which had the deserved reputation of an excellent public school system. Among other things, the research center for Eastman Kodak was located in Kingsport.

I had wonderful parents. My mother was one of those people who was so loving and giving that she found it difficult to ever say no and consequently took on far too much. She was president of numerous organizations in town, ranging from a mental health center to the church library, and eventually she burned herself out. She had a nervous breakdown and developed phobias such as a fear of heights and fear of someone standing behind her. For our family, living a normal life became difficult after that.

This put a good deal of pressure on me because, despite Ellen's help, I found myself doing much of the grocery shopping and other chores. Combined with my heavy involvement with sports, this virtually eliminated any spare time I might have had. I knew that raising four kids on a modest income was never going to be easy for my parents, but obviously, my mother's illness made it a great deal harder for all of us. I loved my family, and even though I was young, I felt a burden of responsibility to them and did what I could to manage things.

My father was a real role model for me. He was promoted from repairing cash registers to selling them. When he traveled around his sales territory, which included coal mining areas of southwest Virginia, on Saturdays, he often took me with him. We went to small Virginia towns like Grundy, Gate City, and Clinch, towns whose tough-sounding names seemed to reflect the desperate lives of the people. Poverty was pandemic in these areas, and the situation in these communities was only exacerbated by the lack of education, leaving miners and their families to live a hand-to-mouth existence. What I saw and experienced on these weekend business trips taught me that getting an education was critical.

Driving around with my dad in his black Ford station wagon with the cash registers in the back was also an education for me. Nothing was easy, and I could see that my dad worked hard—we had no air-conditioning in the vehicle, we hand cranked the windows, and we bumped along rough roads. But most difficult of all was trying to sell an expensive item like a cash register to store owners who were already barely making a living. My dad, I observed, needed to be a very good salesman to be able to make store owners see that the outlay could eventually make them money.

Probably the best life lesson I learned from my father was the way he treated people. It didn't matter whether he was talking to a gas station owner, a convenience store clerk, or a random man in the street; I watched my dad treat every single person with equal respect.

In many cases, my dad also went the extra mile to help people improve their lives. The cash registers he sold enabled store owners to take charge of their businesses, and my dad proved tireless in helping them learn how to manage their money. Frequently, he would come home for our regular family dinner at five thirty p.m., only to leave again an hour later to go back to one of his clients and help to close that client's business for the day. Sometimes, I would go with him on these evenings, and I learned a thing or two about money management myself. I valued these times with my dad and learned from him all the time.

In the poor areas that were part of my father's sales territory, there was a tendency for employees to stick their hand in the till. My dad understood this and found a creative and practical way to help his clients. He made certain a store's owner posted a sign above the cash register, reading, "If you do not receive a receipt, your purchase is free." The employees had to ring up the sale of every item or give it away.

I appreciated my father and what he did for people, and I know others did too. Not too long ago, I received an email from an old acquaintance in Kingsport. His father, Don Fleming, was a big, attractive guy who owned an Esso gas station and had been one of my father's good friends and clients. The email read, "Your dad had more to do with my dad's success than you will ever know, helping keep track of the money. You have no idea how big an impact he had." It was heartwarming to read that and consider the ripple effects of my father's work and care, even some fifty years later.

Outwardly, my dad could appear gruff and tough to people. He was particularly hard on my sister, always pushing her to do better. He set high standards. And he was a major figure in the city, at the First Baptist Church, and on the town council. He often spoke against the grain, like the time when he advocated drilling for oil that had been discovered beneath a park downtown; though that stance did not make him popular or help him get reelected, he was a man who stood for what he thought was right.

Among the most powerful lessons in life I learned from my mom and dad are the importance of family and the incredible value of unconditional love from a parent. I experienced that love. I also watched my father rise above adversities in his life, finding a way to build something good and help others. He was resourceful, hardworking, dedicated, smart, and so much more. He valued respect. He expected a lot, not only of himself but also of others. I'm grateful for the upbringing I had, and though it wasn't always easy in my family, I know I'm the person I am largely due to these early influences.

3

Addison's Disease and the End of My Athletic Dreams

GIVEN MY FAMILY SITUATION WHILE I was growing up, I decided early on that I would pay for my own college education. I knew there was no way my family would be able to afford to send all four kids to college, so I delivered the Knoxville paper and worked every summer, mowing lawns, painting houses, and loading milk trucks at the local PET Dairy. This job probably helped me become a stronger athlete—lifting wooden cartons off the conveyer belt did wonders for the muscles in my thighs and lower back—and I'm pretty sure the hard work and physical conditioning made me an even better basketball player.

Basketball had always been a childhood passion of mine, and I had dreams of playing it in college. But those dreams were never realized, because God giveth and he taketh away, if you believe in such things, which, as a well-brought-up Southern Baptist, I suppose I did.

What I had been given was a strong six-foot, three-inch frame, great leaping ability, and good hand-eye coordination. In high school, my scoring record ensured I got noticed while playing for the Kingsport Indians in East Tennessee. In January 1960, during my junior year, I set a Big 7 Conference record with forty-nine points against Bristol High School (Tennessee). Roy Skinner, the freshman basketball coach at Vanderbilt University, came to recruit me. Interest soared, and Coach Harry Lancaster from the University of Kentucky was in touch, as was Lefty Driesell from Davidson College. The fact that I was a straight-A student helped pique their interest, and my seventeen-point-per-game average that year heightened my prospects of a college scholarship to play basketball. It seemed as if my dreams were within reach.

Then something weird happened. Before my senior year, I started losing weight and losing my ability to jump. I felt my strength draining away. Our family doctor, a Duke University–trained internal medicine specialist, ran all sorts of tests but could not find the answer.

In my last year of high school basketball, I grappled with a growing sense of frustration. The season was tough for me physically, and my contributions seemed to be fading. I was down thirty pounds and could barely make it up and down the court. Though my team produced an amazing 36–3 record that year, we lost in the final game of the state championships.

Then, it got worse. In June 1961, at my high school graduation ceremony, I passed out. My poor parents and my classmates watched in fear as I was carried out on a stretcher. My parents made the tough but necessary decision to take me 300 miles away to Vanderbilt medical school in Nashville.

My body had become emaciated, and my skin had grown dark. Dr. Grant Liddle, a world-renowned endocrinologist at Vanderbilt, saw me not long after I arrived at the hospital. After taking one look at me, he said, "This kid has Addison's disease!" It was a good thing he recognized my condition quickly because it turned out my adrenal glands were not functioning and I was near death. Addison's disease was and is a poorly understood autoimmune condition, but I learned that day that I didn't only have Addison's disease; I also had an extremely rare idiopathic version with an unknown cause. In the way it presented itself, I had a deep tan, and all my pressure points—knuckles, elbows, knees—were black.

Given the rarity of my condition, a large number of Vanderbilt medical students wanted to "see an Addisonian," and so the parade past my hospital bed began. At that stage, I did not realize that another part of my body had been affected quite dramatically by the change in pigmentation. I soon realized that my penis had turned almost completely black. I was a medical curiosity, and for this reason, all the doctors in training wanted to take a peek under my sheets. I'm fairly certain that many nurses paraded through as doctors; either that or the medical school class for that year was predominantly female. As an eighteen-year-old at the time, I was more than embarrassed to show it off.

In the end, the medical solution for me consisted of a daily regimen of hydrocortisone pills, which offered a near-perfect replacement for what my adrenals did not produce. Ever since the summer of 1961, I have lived a normal and active life on a daily administration of hydrocortisone and Florinef, a second drug I needed to maintain the salt balance in my body. I do note that Addison's was a precursor of other autoimmune conditions and several others that have come my way in my lifetime.

On returning home to a summer of recovery, I quickly learned that colleges had lost interest and my hopes of a basketball scholarship had dried up—with one exception. My friend, Coach Roy Skinner at Vanderbilt, persisted and worked with the academic side at Vanderbilt to offer me a half-basketball, half-academic scholarship. This was critical, since I would not have been able to afford Vanderbilt without this support.

That fall, I entered Vanderbilt with a strong freshman basketball crew but quickly saw I was not the player I had been two years earlier. I became the sixth man on the freshman team (yes, we still had freshman teams back then) and scored about four points a game. My dream of playing a starring role in the sport I loved was vanishing. I could see that clearly; the time had come for me to reevaluate my commitment to basketball, and I needed to be realistic.

Late in my freshman year, one long afternoon, I sat alone in the Episcopal chapel a few steps from my fraternity house. I shed lots of tears, sent up loads of prayers, and felt many feelings of anguish as I contemplated giving up my lifelong passion. By the end of the afternoon, I had come to the realization that I had to be strong and move on to a new stage in my life, a stage that I could not yet envision at that time. All I knew was that it was not one that included college basketball.

I did not give up athletics entirely. I became involved with intramural sports, playing football, basketball, and softball for the Pikes, my fraternity. In fact, I was the Vandy Intramural Athlete of the Year in 1963. I still had some game, even if not at the Southeastern Conference level.

But life had changed. And as a believer that all things happen for a reason, I can say that having to give up basketball turned out to be the best thing that happened in my young life.

Vanderbilt Years

4

Learning to Lead

ENDING MY BASKETBALL CAREER FORCED me to think through what I wanted to do next. As I mentioned, I had joined a fraternity at Vanderbilt, becoming a brother of the Sigma chapter of Pi Kappa Alpha, better known as the Pikes. Many of my Pike brothers were active in student politics, particularly my close friend, the late Lee Smith, who had been elected president of the student senate. Lee and others encouraged me to run for the senate. I did so and was elected during my sophomore year.

I wasn't a member of the student senate long before I realized that the oft-used term "the Debating Society" was in fact a proper descriptor for it. I remember being shocked to learn how boring, time-consuming, and seemingly irrelevant to student life the senate actually was. Don't get me wrong—student life itself was exciting and vibrant, but I could see that it was happening in clubs, dorms, fraternities, sororities, and sports programs, not in the senate.

I became disillusioned with the senate and, wanting to see if we could do better, began to come up with an idea. It seemed to me that the best forum for student representation might not be through the senate but instead through a new board of presidents, representing the clubs and organizations we all belonged to, cared about, and worked so hard to make relevant. Midway through my junior year, I ran for president of the Student Government Association (SGA) on a platform that surprised many. Since it was clear that the only way to get rid of the student senate would be to get it to vote itself out of existence, I made that my campaign pledge: "Elect Michael Ainslie President of SGA, and he will abolish the Student Senate." That was one of the first opportunities in my life to identify a problem, "see things the way they are not," and then sell a "big idea." I really enjoyed getting others excited about sharing a vision.

My good friend Tom Amonett was my opponent, and he did well, particularly among the guys, winning the male vote by a slim margin. However, I had a secret weapon. Ruthie Montgomery, my girlfriend at the time, was incredibly well liked and well organized, and largely through her leadership and our joint efforts, we won the female vote by a sizeable margin. I won the election by offering a clear vision of a better approach to student government. It taught me that going against established ideas can be rewarded if your new idea is a better one and is delivered with clarity.

As the new president, I got to work right away on fulfilling my campaign promise and figuring how to abolish the senate. I realized the enormous challenge I was up against: I needed to form a coalition that would be compelling to the twenty-eight senators and needed to convince them to fire themselves!

I created my SGA cabinet with leaders from all over the campus, enlisting my good friend Herschel Bloom from Zeta Beta Tau and the Intrafraternity Council, the president of the Honor Council, other presidents of fraternities and sororities, leaders of residence halls, and more. The cabinet and I worked tirelessly over the summer, with my attorney general taking the lead in putting together a constitution for the new board of presidents. Amazingly, my plan worked, and in the spring of 1965, after much debate, the student senate voted 24–4 to abolish itself and be replaced by a new board of presidents.

This model must have had some merit. For the next twenty years or so, it was the form of representative government at Vanderbilt University. Then, as luck would have it, some other bright young SGA president convinced people that a student senate was needed, and it came back into existence.

I believe this experience was an invaluable part of my growing up. I gained a great deal of confidence from bringing about the redesign of Vanderbilt student government and in my ability to achieve real change against great odds. I became instilled with the belief that people could be convinced of any good idea, no matter how radical it appeared. It took careful planning, the building of a strong coalition of other respected leaders, and a lot of late-night conversations with members of the student senate. But going forward, I discovered that accomplishing real change was not nearly as daunting a task for me. And much of my later effectiveness with The Posse Foundation, Sotheby's, and the National Trust for Historic Preservation can be attributed directly to this early success.

Traveling the World
in My Twenties

5

Expanding My Worldview

AS I NEARED MY GRADUATION from Vanderbilt, I had no clue what might be my next chapter. Fortunately, at that time, I had been given a cushy part-time job, known as the dean's messenger. It took only a few hours every day or so but gave me a chance to become close to John Bingham, the arts and sciences dean. Dean Bingham urged me to apply for the Corning Foundation World Travel Fellowship.

Since I'd never been overseas, the idea of a year of international travel was highly appealing to me. I had grown up as a conservative southerner, experiencing little of the outside world, but I knew a lot was out there, and I wanted to see it. For my fellowship application, I wrote a theoretical proposal of economic development, detailing a study of cartels in Europe and zaibatsu (family business combinations) in Japan. That and my leadership track record were good enough to help me be selected for the fellowship.

The Corning Fellowship was made possible by Amory Houghton Jr., chairman of the board of Corning Glass Works, a company that, since its founding in 1851, has been at the forefront of glass innovation. Corning developed the glass used in fiber optics; Pyrex; Pyroceram, the glass used for ceramic cookware and for the nose cone of rockets; and most recently "gorilla glass" used on Apple iPhones. Amory Houghton, better known as Amo, was approached by Leslie Rollins, the dean of admissions at Harvard Business School (HBS). Together, they shared a vision of the need to expand a college graduate's understanding of the world.

Rollins proposed that they create the Corning Fellowship specifically for Charlie Ravenel, a 1961 graduate of Harvard, to give him the opportunity to visit as many foreign countries as he liked on a self-designed year of travel and study, unfettered by classroom restrictions or instruction. Houghton and Rollins felt other postgraduate fellowships at the time were slanted heavily toward the brilliant academic performer while neglecting "doers" whose contributions to campus life might have had a negative effect on grade averages; these included people such as scholar athletes, SGA officers, and campus newspaper editors. Rollins wanted these students to travel far and wide so that they could witness firsthand how other people lived. The goal was to expand the traveling fellow's leadership experience by having the fellow interview leaders and everyday folks around the world.

Several months after Ravenel departed on the inaugural Corning Fellowship in the fall of 1961, a picture of Ravenel and Indian prime minister Nehru appeared in *Newsweek* on the steps of parliament in New Delhi. Houghton called Dean Rollins at HBS and exclaimed, "It worked."

Quickly, the Corning Fellowship program was expanded from Harvard to include Yale, North Carolina, Kentucky, and Vanderbilt. David Albright was selected as Vanderbilt's first traveling fellow, and I was fortunate enough to follow him two years later upon my graduation in 1965. I went off in the fall of 1965 to change my outlook on the world.

Feeling like a bird out of a cage, I spent $1,300 of my $5,000 grant on a Pan Am round-the-world ticket, and by the time it was all over, I had visited nearly thirty countries, interviewed hundreds of people, and become a citizen of the world. These experiences allowed me to grasp something more of the complexities of different cultures and societies, and to say that my eyes were opened doesn't begin to describe the extent to which I grew as a person during my travels.

There was no curriculum—my instruction was simply to travel wherever I wanted, interview people, and explore. And that was what I did from

Germany, Denmark, and Sweden to France, Czechoslovakia, and Russia. I went to Syria, Kenya, India, Nepal, Burma, Vietnam, and perhaps another fifteen countries.

There was no support on this trip. Unless a person was lucky enough to have a buddy traveling with them—on my trip, Jim Light, the Chapel Hill Corning Fellow, traveled with me for approximately a quarter of the time—they were on their own, discovering what a scary, daunting, inspiring, and extraordinary place the world could be.

In a year, I gathered enough memories to last a lifetime and learned enough lessons to help shape my future career in business and entrepreneurship.

...

JIM AND I STARTED our trip in Europe, where I bought a Volkswagen Beetle. Not wishing to make life easy for ourselves, we drove due north, all the way through Scandinavia, into the Arctic Circle and, turning east, eventually hit the most remote, frozen, deserted border crossing into the Soviet Union that existed anywhere. This was the winter of 1965, and the Cold War was at its height.

As we approached the checkpoint, we could see that there were two Russian soldiers on duty, both toting machine guns. They could have sprayed bullets at 360 degrees and not hit anyone . . . except us. Since I spoke a little German, we were able to have some form of communication with them.

After checking our papers, they started inspecting the car. One of them flipped the back seat down and rummaged around our bags. Almost immediately, he came across the London Fog raincoat I had folded up and placed on the back seat. My heart began to pound because I knew what was in one of the pockets, and I knew there might be dire consequences if the soldier found it; I had heard stories of people who upset the Soviet authorities, including one story of an American student who had been sent to prison in Siberia for stealing an icon, a small work of art. I watched as the soldier now began to examine my raincoat, and when his hands came to rest on the outside of a pocket that contained a wad of rubles I'd bought on the black market in New York (black-market rubles at that time cost only 10% of the official exchange rate), I knew I had to do something.

"*Halte!*" I shouted suddenly, with such force that the soldier jumped and grabbed his machine gun. Quickly, I added, "*Ich habe ein geschenk für dich!*" which means, "I have a present for you!" I didn't know where the thought came from, but I knew I had to come up with an idea fast. Curious, the soldier waited for me to walk around to the trunk where I nervously pulled out a magazine and flipped it open. Then I clutched it to my chest as I walked back toward him, turned it around, and thrust it toward him. It was a *Playboy*, and he found himself staring at the nude centerfold Bunny of the Month. So the soldiers forgot all about the raincoat and waved us into the Soviet Union.

Buying the rubles on the black market was at a minimum youthful naïveté, or some would say stupidity. However, I learned that when faced with a dangerous opponent, you must be quick-witted and that you must create a major distraction to refocus the opponent's attention.

...

TRAVELING THROUGH THE COUNTRYSIDE of Eastern Europe, we noticed that gas stations were few and far between, and the roads were often little more than mud tracks, which left the Beetle mud splattered. Jim and I checked into an Intourist (Soviet tourist agency) hotel in Minsk—now the capital of Belarus but then part of the Soviet Union—and tried to survive on a diet of only borscht, a beet soup that can be tasty but not when it's made largely of water. (Never mind that my stomach didn't agree with it and I got dysentery, which presented a challenge all of its own.)

As we were departing the hotel, I "borrowed" a washcloth, if it could be described as such—it was essentially a worn-out rag, a flimsy piece of fabric with all the cotton tattered—to clean up the poor Beetle. With difficulty, we managed to use the washcloth to wipe the windows clear of the mud, snow, and ice that had accumulated. We had just started to drive off when a large woman in an apron appeared and slammed the hotel's gates closed. She pointed up to a window where we found the regional head of Intourist shouting at us for having stolen the rag. "You must pay fifteen dollars!" he yelled. I was furious and about to fire something back, but Jim tugged at my arm and suggested it was probably best we pay. I realized he was right, given our situation, and we drove off, resenting the needless hole in our meager budget.

...

ONCE WE REACHED POLAND, I noted a distinct difference in the way farming was being conducted. Whereas the Soviet Union had a rigidly applied system of collective farming, completely state controlled, the Poles had somehow managed to resist this, and as a result farms were still privately owned. The farms we saw in Poland appeared to be hives of activity with donkeys pulling carts laden with produce. By contrast, their Soviet equivalents looked sad and lifeless.

At a quick glance, the scenes seemed to back up the heated arguments I'd had in recent days with professors at Moscow University concerning the benefits of rewarding individuals, even within a collective system, through the use of incentives. The professors had vehemently disagreed with me, but here, in Poland, was clear evidence that economic vitality could be produced by incentives.

Once we reached Warsaw, I made excellent use of a contact I had been given by Vanderbilt—David Halberstam, the Pulitzer Prize–winning journalist who had been pulled out of Vietnam after telling his *New York Times* readers what the State Department didn't want them to know about the war. Halberstam had been reassigned by the *Times* to Poland, where he met and fell in love with the leading Polish actress Elżbieta

Czyżewska. He was hospitable to us, and through him we got to meet all manner of interesting people. As we conducted our interviews, it became clear that the Catholic Church still had a powerful hold over the populace and that Communism had not taken hold there to anything like the extent it had in Russia.

...

AFTER TRAVELING ON TO Czechoslovakia and Austria, Jim and I took a civilized pit stop for a few weeks in Zurich, Switzerland, where Corning offered us a chance to work in its European headquarters. Corning Europe was then headed by Jamie Houghton, the younger brother of Amo Houghton. Jamie put us to work doing market research, a pleasant change from the youth hostels and long, lonely days setting up interviews in difficult places. In fact, the whole time in Switzerland offered a stark contrast to what we had been experiencing in Eastern Europe. On weekends, we learned to ski from two wonderful Swiss coworkers, Ursula Gambert and Nini Kundig, from the Corning office. We had nice hotel rooms, an office and desks, a telephone, and access to a typewriter; I think there was even a fax. It all seems quite quaint now, but this was the cutting edge of communication in those days, and I remember taking advantage of the facilities by writing my application for Harvard Business School during that pit stop.

While I was there, I also arranged to have the Volkswagen shipped home, in the hope that my father could sell it. But it proved difficult, and by the time he did, I had no profit on the deal.

...

I MOVED ON FROM Zurich on my own, and several weeks later, Jim and I met up again in Cairo. We set out on a trip down the Nile and took the train to Luxor and the construction site of the future Aswan Dam. On our way back, my stomach started playing up again—a fact we mentioned to the nice gentleman sitting opposite us who turned out to be a colonel in the Egyptian Army. Colonel Hassan Serry, who instructed us to call him Foxy, had been educated at Sandhurst, Britain's equivalent of West Point, and exuded an attractive mix of British bearing and Egyptian charm; he had been head of the royal guards under King Farouk and was lucky to have survived Nasser's overthrow of Farouk in 1952. Being hospitable, Foxy invited us to spend a few nights at his family apartment when we reached Cairo, which was a huge relief for me. He even took us to see belly dancing at the Auberge des Pyramides, King Farouk's favorite haunt and the hottest nightclub in Cairo.

Michael Ainslie and Jim Light in Cairo at the Auberge des Pyramides
nightclub with Zizette Serry and her father, Colonel Hassan "Foxy" Serry,
and her brother Mustaffa Serry, April 1966.

There turned out to be a far more lasting benefit because Foxy had a daughter named Zizette, who became a lifelong friend. My wife Suzanne and I have come to know Zizette's children and grandchildren. They have visited us at our home in Florida, and we, in turn, enjoyed a wonderful dinner with them in Cairo in 2010, only months before the 2011 revolution. I have connected many traveling fellows with the Serry family over the fifty years of our friendship.

...

AFRICA, WITH ITS VISTAS, wildlife, and tribal families living their lives in a fashion so far removed from anything I had ever known, was an experience that widened my perception of our universe. It was unforgettable to me. During my travels, I went to Kenya and then crossed, for a time, into Tanzania, taking a local bus from Arusha to reach the Ngorongoro Crater, one of the world's largest craters, 2,000 feet deep and covering 102 square miles. While there, I ran into a group of Pan Am flight attendants who let me hitch a ride in their chartered Land Rover through the crater.

The crater contained every species of animal that lives in Africa. While there, I stayed at a youth hostel on the rim of the crater and remember one day going to see how the other half lived at the fancy Rim Lodge a mile away. At dusk, not being able to find a ride back to my hostel, I decided to hike back on my own. I encountered many alarming creatures on that trek, including a huge wildebeest, a snorting elephant, and secretary birds with enormously long feathers. I was scared but also felt the beat of Africa with every step. On finally reaching the hostel, I was greeted by a wide-eyed African boy. "You are very brave!" he exclaimed, which made me realize my walk home had not been so much brave but stupid. Innocence is bliss, however, because although I was lucky to be alive, the experience was amazing.

It was great fun to travel back to Ngorongoro Crater in December 2018, and this time, I was able to afford to stay at the Rim Lodge. I regaled Suzanne, Serena (our daughter), and the two other families with whom we traveled with stories of my survival from my trip more than fifty years earlier.

...

WHEN I VISITED KENYA, I received one of my great learnings in life. At the time—1966—Jomo Kenyatta, who was president of Kenya from independence in 1963 to 1978, was still in his early years of presidency and facing a coup from a political opponent known locally as "Double O." Kenyatta came from the largest tribal community in Kenya, the Kikuyu, whereas Double O, Oginga Odinga, was a Luo, the second-largest tribal community in Kenya. Caught with a warehouse full of Chinese weapons, Double O was taken into custody, and it was clear that his planned coup had the potential of creating a bloody tribal civil war in Kenya.

While today, the political crisis in Kenya features a Kenyatta and an Odinga, showing how the tribes and many of the same families still rule in Kenya, back in 1966, Kenyatta, I believe, made a brilliant political move. Rather than imprison Double O for his planned coup, Kenyatta reorganized the government and made Double O the head of a province in far western Kenya, removing him from influence in Nairobi and avoiding a bloody war that might have resulted from a more draconian response. It was powerful and eye-opening for me to be in Kenya around this time, and from it I learned that sometimes in life the best reaction to a problem is to do the least obvious thing and the least disruptive.

I was fascinated by this and spent my three weeks in East Africa asking scores of people about the leadership style of Kenyatta and his counterpart in Tanzania, Julius Nyerere. It was an incredible opportunity to learn, and I found the insights I gained there particularly helpful. Later, I was able to apply some of these same lessons when I was heading Sotheby's.

...

I NEEDED QUITE A bit of patience to get into Israel. Even though I had my visa, I got no farther than the Mandelbaum Gate on my first attempt. The Mandelbaum is the main entry point from Jordan into Jerusalem, and with proper documents, entry should have been routine. But one needs to deal with the human factor at every checkpoint, literal or imagined, in the Middle East, and the Jordanian official there wouldn't let me pass. Despite my protestations, I was told to come back the next day. On a tight budget, I knew that this would mean an extra night's accommodation I wasn't prepared for.

I was barred from entry again the next day, and it eventually took me three days to get through. When I asked why, the Jordanian officer replied, "You must understand, we hate these people." The incident provided me with an unpleasant close-up of the age-old enmities that existed then and, unhappily, still exist today.

In spite of my early difficulties, my time in the Middle East began with an incredible two weeks with an old Vanderbilt friend, Johnny Jones, who was spending a year before medical school teaching at American University in Beirut. In those days, Beirut was the garden spot of the region, full of sheiks zooming around in their Mercedes and Maseratis. Jones had a Honda motorcycle and, from a friend, borrowed a second one for me to ride during a long weekend trip we took to the Gulf of Aqaba. Having never before ridden a motorcycle, I found it to be a daunting experience.

It was the spring of 1966, and in Syria, the Baath revolution had just occurred. Though Russian tanks with machine-gun-toting soldiers were everywhere when we arrived in Damascus, we got through unscathed but a bit rattled.

We rode on toward Petra, and during this part of the trip, my motorcycle inexperience caught up with me. The curvy road leading in to Petra had gravel alongside it, and as I attempted to keep up with Jones, it grabbed me. My Honda slid out from under me, and I went flying over the handlebars, rolling through the desert like a rag doll. As I looked back in the dust, I realized how fortunate I had been. Large boulders were everywhere, and I had somehow managed to roll down the only straight line there was. Scraped a bit but with no serious injuries, I got up and returned to my bike to find the handlebar snapped off at the center knuckle. I rode the next fifty miles holding the busted half of the handlebar in my lap until we were able to find a welding shop to fix the damage.

All things considered, we saw the incredible Rose-Red City of Rock, as Petra is known, and then headed south toward Jerusalem. We enjoyed an amazing overnight there and also a walk at dawn through the ancient city, where we were drawn to a primitive bakery by the enticing smell of fresh-baked bread. We also rode down to spend an afternoon swimming in the Gulf of Aqaba.

Since the heat of the desert had been causing my motorcycle chain to stretch and keep slipping, I returned to Jerusalem to get it fixed. Jones needed to get back to Beirut to teach his course, so I rode back alone a day later. Upon arrival, I was shocked to learn that my friend had not made it back. It turned out that he was in jail in Damascus where he'd naively stopped to snap a picture of a Russian tank. A soldier leapt off the tank, took him to the ground, and accused him of being an American journalist, marching him off to jail. Only after they developed his photos and saw the two of us floating in the nude (bathing suits were not in our backpacks) in the Dead Sea did they realize he might be telling the truth about being a poor teacher in Beirut and finally released him.

...

DURING MY YEAR OF travels, I also made my way to India, where I got to meet politician I. K. Gujral, a leader of India's Congress Party. (Gujral would become India's prime minister many years later in 1997.) At the time, the US government had been using its excess US wheat production for a food aid program called the PL 480 Food for Peace. India had been receiving large quantities of wheat under this program when I learned that suddenly and without warning, the US Congress decided to sharply reduce the program; the United States then issued a mandate to India, informing India that it needed to build a fertilizer plant quickly or lose the wheat it had been receiving.

With an amazing bit of candor to a twenty-three-year-old American traveler, Gujral explained to me, "In the following election, we lost control of Parliament because of our quick approval of an AMOCO fertilizer plant under duress from your government." It was difficult and upsetting for me to witness the misuse of American power in such an up close way. I felt we had the right to tell India to become more self-sufficient in producing more grain for its people, but to force India to build a fertilizer plant was way beyond a reasonable use of our government's power.

· · ·

THOUGH I WAS EXPERIENCING some of the greatest adventures of my life up to that point, I also knew my eyes had been opened even more to injustice, poverty, oppression, corruption, and abuse of power. These were things my eyes couldn't unsee, and at the same time that these created conflict in me, I didn't want to forget them. I continued to carry the images, stories, and lessons of my travels with me, and I still do.

6

Corkscrew Landing in Vietnam

AMONG OTHER COUNTRIES I VISITED during my year as a Corning Fellow, Vietnam was a place that left a long and lasting impression on me. In the spring of 1966, I found myself in Southeast Asia at the height of the Vietnam War and got the first whiff of it when I ventured up to the northeast corner of Thailand near the Laotian border. In Bangkok, I met a Peace Corps worker who was in the hospital receiving treatment for STDs. He invited me to travel to Sakon Nakhon, the village where he lived, and I decided to go.

Upon our arrival at his village, he introduced me to the local mayor. This Peace Corps worker taught English to the mayor's kids, and in return, the mayor had given him a comfortable house. Not too far away, the Vietcong were operating just over the Mekong River, the great artery of Southeast Asia, and the mayor told me that the Vietcong had threatened to kill his children if he did not do everything they asked of him. He had become a Vietcong puppet out of fear. "These are bad people," he told me, and I was not about to argue.

Moving on through Cambodia, I eventually arrived in Saigon, as it was then known (today, it's Ho Chi Minh City), and got a close-up view of the impact the war was having on South Vietnam's capital. US military personnel were everywhere, their trucks and jeeps weaving through endless streams of local cyclists and young men on scooters with their girlfriends clinging to their waists. In addition to the military, there was also a large expatriate community; I quickly came to realize that many expats follow global disturbances, like the Vietnam War. Taken all together, it was quite a wild scene.

The air was hot and sticky on my first night there, so I went in search of a cool drink at the bar of the blissfully air-conditioned Caravelle Hotel. Within minutes, I fell into conversation with the personnel director of RMK-BRJ, the conglomerate doing all the construction for the US military. The task at hand was a huge and challenging one, and he was not holding back on the Jack Daniels as he described it to me.

"The stupid embassy people don't have a clue," he muttered to me. Then he began to reveal the biggest source of his troubles: "The cost of living has tripled in the past eighteen months, and my people can't live on what they are getting. I need an economist to present the facts to the idiots over at the embassy." It was not a small problem he was describing. He had 50,000 employees to look after, consisting of 40,000 Vietnamese employees, 5,000 South Korean employees, and 5,000 American expats. He needed help.

And there I was, a totally inexperienced young man, rapidly running out of money in a war zone far from home *but* with an economics degree from Vanderbilt University. I presented myself to this personnel director as a Vanderbilt-trained economist and, after another Jack Daniels, was hired on the spot. Earning $1,600 a month sounded mighty good at that point, given that I had almost nothing left of my fellowship grant.

The next day I found myself working with Peter Ritson, a Cal Berkeley graduate. Our brief was to prevent the threatened strike and negotiate a wage settlement, but I nearly didn't last the course. I jumped in a taxi, which I recall was a Deux Chevaux, the flimsy little Citroën that was the cheapest car on the market in those days, and set off on my first order of business to get a medical exam. Along the way, I ran into a demonstration of Buddhist monks, one of whom had just set himself on fire in protest to the war. I barely had time to respond before my driver and I were swallowed by an angry mob. With our small car sur-rounded, demonstrators quickly saw that I was a Westerner and within seconds started beating furiously on the car, rocking it violently and making motions that indicated they were going to turn it over, which would not at all have been difficult to do. I managed to get the driver to reverse quickly and take me immediately back to my hotel. I had never been more petrified in my life, and my first instinct that day was to get the hell out of Vietnam on the next available flight. I did everything I could but was informed by the airline that the next available seat was two weeks away. So I stayed and went to work.

The conditions were volatile, made worse by the tensions and pres-sures of the war. Peter and I needed to find a solution for the labor unrest, already an emotionally charged situation that had been prompted by a lack of adequate pay for workers. Things erupted only a few days later when the entire RMK workforce went on strike. This was a huge problem for the US military because it was awaiting the completion of ports, airstrips, roads, and other facilities to carry out the war.

Suddenly Ritson and Ainslie became the labor negotiating team rep-resenting 40,000 Vietnamese construction workers. Hard to believe, but it was true. The negotiations began with us sitting across the table from many US embassy and State Department folks. We were at it for nine-ty-six hours in a mammoth negotiating session and literally did not sleep for four days. Everyone was acutely aware of the need to come up with a settlement.

The settlement was incredibly complicated, particularly since there were hundreds of different categories of employees. In the end, we finally settled on a pay raise of 25% for most of the employees, which was still grossly inadequate considering how rapidly food prices had been rising, but we had to get the show back on the road. Though we reached a set-tlement, many job categories unfortunately got less and others got more, since the US Army generals did not want RMK to pay more than they did for the Vietnamese working to build their personal villas for them.

Our efforts were not universally popular, and I didn't relish the thought of my next task, which was to explain the settlement—and the reasons for it—to the project managers spread all over Vietnam. To accomplish this, I was given a pilot and a Beechcraft Baron, a light, twin-engine piston aircraft. I set off to the twenty jobsites north of Saigon, all of which were located in active war zones—places like Cam Rahn Bay, Danang, Pleiku, all made famous by the Vietnam War.

There I was as a twenty-three-year-old, explaining our settlement to a seasoned construction boss at each jobsite. However, I did think at one point that my journey was going to be fatally interrupted when my pilot had to make a corkscrew landing in order to keep us alive. Pleiku, our destination at that time, was a hilltop encampment where some of the fiercest fighting of the war took place, and the pilot needed to bring us down in a way that minimized our risk of getting hit by incoming fire. Our Baron lost an engine coming in to land at Pleiku, but my Air America pilot seemed unconcerned in his gung-ho sort of way. "We can land these things on one engine—no problem!" he insisted. But with just a hint of sarcasm, he commented, "It might be a really big problem if we lose it on takeoff tomorrow morning!"

We made it in and out of Pleiku in one piece, but I believe it worth mentioning that Air America pilots were among the unsung heroes of the war. Working for an airline run by the CIA, they ferried VIPs and cargo all over South Vietnam during the war, often in highly dangerous situations. Never would I have guessed when I was first awarded the Corning Fellowship that I would wind up in Vietnam doing a corkscrew landing in a small plane to avoid being shot down, and all this for a job in which I was an advocate for 40,000 workers.

I am sure my parents would have had heart failure had they known what I was up to in Vietnam during my year abroad. I did not mention the riot I was in or the war zones I passed through. Fortunately, social media did not yet exist, and my snail mail letters home did not provide them with the scary details.

...

IN THE END, THE more I witnessed of the war, the more disillusioned I became. The stuff that was going on was, to me, both unbelievable and disconcerting. I learned through RMK meetings of $300 million worth of trucks and material being stolen off the landing vessels. The Vietcong, who could not be distinguished from our own Vietnamese employees, would meet the landing craft and drive off into the forest with much of the cargo, which would immediately be used in the war against us.

I began to understand more of the limitations of American power that existed behind the propaganda headlines. We needed more David Halberstams in the field, telling the story as it really was. Instead, I saw agency reporters duty-bound to report the exaggerations on offer during what the press corps dubbed "the Five O'Clock Follies"—the ritual 5:00 p.m. press briefing that was carried out each day at the Military Assistance Command, Vietnam, headquarters in Saigon. I knew, to put it mildly, that the briefing officers were not telling the whole story.

I departed Vietnam after three months, feeling that the United States was making a big mistake in being involved in the war. What I saw and experienced there changed me, which, I realized soon afterward, was the point of my travel fellowship. The goal of the Corning program was to give young people the chance to learn through travel, interviews, and conversations with people in other cultures and societies. It was an incredible experience through which I learned a lot about not only the world but also myself.

Today, Vanderbilt is the only one of the five original universities to offer the program that still gives a fellowship. Over the years, several of us, including David Albright, Ed Turner, Jud Pankey, Dr. Kelly Moore, Michael Keegan, and I, have worked hard to raise funds and to continue the program. It is now known as the Keegan Traveling Fellowship, since Michael Keegan, the fellow from 1980, endowed the program some years back. Each spring we give a $20,000 grant to two graduating seniors and send them off as Keegan Fellows to see the world. Interestingly, two-thirds of the fellows have been women in the past twenty years, whereas the first thirty years saw mostly men win the award. A fiftieth fellows reunion held in 2013 was a special time to hear about the incredible impact the year of travel has had on the lives of the fellows who gathered. It certainly expanded my worldview, informed my thinking in work and life, and made me a better person.

I have discovered that life's lessons are best learned on the hoof. Sometimes that entails quick thinking, sometimes ingenuity, and sometimes patience. Perhaps the best lesson from my year on the Corning Fellowship is the realization that we are all, no matter our homeland, so similar. We want our community to be a place where we can learn, grow, have friends and family that are safe and happy, and yet so many forces often pull against these values. Governments, including our own, often don't reinforce these values. They can make it difficult to achieve our dreams. It made me want to do all I could to help in small ways in my daily interactions with individuals and in bigger ways through improving relations among organizations and even between countries as I was able to do in my years at Sotheby's.

As an example, I remember senior officials in South Korea not wanting Sotheby's to open an office in Seoul, claiming that we would be plundering their art and taking it out of their country. I explained that on the contrary we would be sending them catalogs in advance of every global auction that included Korean objects. They would be able to repatriate works of art that had left Korea. In fact, a year after they finally allowed us to open, an important Korean prayer tapestry appeared in our Milan, Italy, sale, and by having early notification, a Korean buyer was able to purchase it and donate it to a museum in South Korea. They were thrilled and became supporters of Sotheby's in South Korea.

Career Beginnings

7

Death Threats in New York City

BETWEEN MY TWO YEARS AT Harvard Business School, I was lucky to get a summer associate position at McKinsey & Company, one of the world's top and most influential management consulting firms. At the time, a job at McKinsey was, as it is today, a plum position. I found the work there exciting and engaging, and when, following graduation, I was offered a full-time job with the company, I took it.

While I had a higher-paying offer from Boston Consulting Group, the attraction of the urban practice at McKinsey was compelling. This was 1968, and America was in Vietnam-induced turmoil. Riots were taking place in Watts in Los Angeles, in Chicago, and in many other cities. Martin Luther King Jr. was assassinated on April 4, 1968. The climate in the United States was explosive, I was troubled by it, and I wanted to do my bit to help solve some of these societal problems.

I had an MBA from Harvard, but I have often referred to my time at McKinsey as my PhD in business. Those years gave me a great education in how to deal with people and think strategically. My first two years at McKinsey saw me redesigning program delivery systems for Housing and Urban Development and its urban renewal program and working on rent-controlled housing in New York City and on several corporate projects. I found that I was good at consulting and enjoyed the challenge of leading different teams. Little did I know my involvement in one key project would lead to death threats against me in which a judge would have to warn me that "Get Ainslie" was the word on the street.

I had been leading a McKinsey team trying to make sense of Model Cities, a federal program created by President Lyndon Johnson in an attempt to improve services in the country's toughest big-city neighborhoods. New York received $65 million a year for this initiative in the poverty-stricken communities of the South Bronx, East Harlem, and Bedford-Stuyvesant. The first administrator of this program in New York, Eugenia Flatow, had taken the community control admonition so seriously that she allowed community boards to fragment the money into scores of new small programs, which resulted in little to no impact in these communities at all. New York City Mayor John Lindsay fired Flatow as administrator and instead appointed Judge J. B. Williams, a bright African American family court judge from Brooklyn, to try and revive the still young but struggling program. Judge Williams immediately asked who knew the most about Model Cities and was told by Mayor Lindsay's aide that he needed to meet Michael Ainslie, a consultant from McKinsey who had been trying to rationalize the program to increase its impact.

At the time, I was in a New Hampshire hospital, having just shattered my right hip from a late-afternoon fall into an icy creek while skiing. Fortunately, a good surgeon pinned my hip back together, and a few days later, I was in an ambulance heading to the Drake Hotel in New York where, from a prone position on a couch, I briefed Judge Williams on the intricacies of Model Cities. He liked what he heard and asked if I would become his deputy. The plan was for me to run the day-to-day operations of the program while he went to the streets to buy us some time from the community, where he had great credibility and respect as a judge. (Williams would, some years later, be appointed to the New York State Supreme Court.) I liked Judge Williams, believed in his approach, and thought I could contribute something of value to his team, so I agreed to take a leave of absence from McKinsey.

Hobbling around on crutches, I led the effort to concentrate the

program's dollars into a few visible high-impact programs such as affordable housing, vacant lot clearance, and improved ambulance response
time. But doing this meant that other programs could not be supported;
community leaders whose pet programs were eliminated became infuri-
ated. Their anger culminated in the "Get Ainslie" death threats I heard
from Judge Williams as we prepared to head off to a tough weekend pro-
gramming session.

"I hear the South Bronx guys are packing their rods. Are you certain
you want to show up?" Judge Williams asked me on the morning that
we were departing for this important retreat. The community boards of
the three New York Model Cities neighborhoods would be present at this
retreat, and though I didn't know about the death threats against me until
my boss warned me, I had felt the tension rising in previous weeks.

I must say my nose for trouble was twitching quite a bit when I heard
this, but I knew the good we could do in the community and I didn't want
to give up. "If I don't show up, I am through at Model Cities forever," I
said to Judge Williams. Deciding to take the risk, I went to meet the community boards, and while it was a fractious weekend, I'm glad to report
that no weapons appeared.

Sadly, our efforts to realize material change in these impoverished
neighborhoods were not successful. While we achieved some success in
small ways, the problems were too systemic to be eradicated with money
and program redesign. I learned how fundamental our urban challenges
are. Clearly, my later involvement with The Posse Foundation grew from
this experience. Education is the best answer, and I put my full energies
into giving talented young urban leaders a real chance to change things.

Another lesson was learned from the time I spent running Model Cities under the administration of Mayor John Lindsay and under the direction of my boss and friend, Judge J. B. Williams. This experience allowed
me to gain some additional insight into what I wanted to do and what
I was good at in life. In spite of the death threats, I realized I could see
through the status quo of a situation and create some real change in the

world. I loved the challenge of building a team, shaping a strategy, and making decisions that I then had to live with. I realized I was okay with a degree of risk. And though McKinsey asked me to stay on with the hope of becoming a partner after I ended my work with the Model Cities program, I knew then that consulting would not ultimately be fulfilling for me. After a great three years with McKinsey, it was time for me to find a job running something.

I'm grateful for McKinsey and the high caliber of talent and quality of people there. I appreciated the way it could inform and improve the critical work of teams and initiatives in not only private but also public sectors. Under the leadership of a young partner named Carter Bales in the late '60s, McKinsey had built an urban affairs practice to help mayors and government agencies improve their decision making and service delivery. At the time, Mayor Lindsay, his budget director Frederick O'Reilly Hayes, and a brain trust of young aides, including Peter Goldmark, Jay Kriegel, and Gordon Davis, recognized this McKinsey talent and placed project teams all over city government. Though Lindsay's chief rival, Comptroller Abraham Beame, made this a big political issue, eventually forcing Lindsay to phase out McKinsey's involvement since McKinsey's fees were substantially more than normal government salaries, I felt McKinsey made major contributions to improving the effectiveness of many New York City programs and agencies.

My time at McKinsey was pivotal in my personal growth and was filled with good and long-lasting friendships. Ron Daniel was the partner who recruited me. He went on to become a McKinsey legend, heading the firm worldwide. He built long-standing client relationships and became a role model for me and many others. Ron also later became Harvard's treasurer and served on the boards of Brandeis, the National Trust, and many other leading nonprofits. As a personal aside, I want to note that Ron is a really good golfer and a member of the Augusta National Golf Club. I share one of my greatest golfing memories with him when, over two days of play as his guest at Augusta, I made natural birdies on all four of the par five holes, even watching one ball dive into the hole forty feet from where I was putting, in an amazing birdie fest that I, to this day, still call the Ainslie Grand Slam of Golf.

Carter Bales remained a friend until his recent passing. With a passion for solving complex problems, he spent most of his career at McKinsey and then formed the NewWorld Capital Group, a fund investing in environmentally and socially responsible ventures. After I later moved on to work with Sotheby's, we stayed in touch, and his late wife Susie, also a dear and wonderful friend, got Suzanne and me involved with the Graham School, the oldest childcare agency in America. Through that friendship and connection, Suzanne and I had the opportunity to work hard to raise $4 million to restore a campus for homeless and abused kids in Hastings on the Hudson in New York. We were able to get Arthur Ashe to help us raise funds for two tennis courts, and he came to give a clinic for the Graham kids at the groundbreaking. It was a most rewarding involvement. I'm thankful for this friendship with a former McKinsey alumnus who demonstrated to me how one can tackle, if not completely solve, complex urban issues.

Out of this season of my life, I enjoyed another connection. When Suzanne and I, many years later, moved to Palm Beach in 1998, a neighbor from across the street showed up at our front door as we were still unboxing our things. I remember peering out the door to find a tall, elegant gal. She inquired, "Does Suzy Hooker live here?" "Well, yes," I responded, "but you and I are the only two people who know she was once called Suzy Hooker." It turns out this neighbor was the daughter of Mayor John Lindsay and had also been a classmate and close friend of Suzanne's when they attended the Chapin School in New York together. Margi Lindsay Picotte; her husband, Michael; and their three wonderful kids became some of our best friends and remain so. Margi is a world-class putter, and Suzanne and I have played golf together all over the world with Margi and Michael. (Unfortunately for Michael and me, our wives always win.)

I greatly value the McKinsey and Model Cities phase of my life. McKinsey taught me how to write cogently, how to tear apart a balance sheet, and how to understand what was really going on in an organization. Model Cities called on me to further hone my skills at building up people, to execute on difficult plans, and to step into risk to do something worthwhile. In so many ways, these experiences prepared me for a career path that I today define as nonlinear.

I would go on to work in a number of different fields and sectors, including luxury real estate, fertilizer, and historic preservation; unbeknownst to me at the time, I'd also later join the leadership of Sotheby's and Lehman Brothers. My nose for trouble followed me into each and every space. Some people, commenting on the weird wanderings of my career path, have referred to my journey as "From chic to shit and back again." It may have been. These experiences weren't always easy, but they made me stronger, smarter, and better, trouble and all. I deeply cherish each and every one of them, and best of all, I never got bored.

Work and Life
in Puerto Rico

8

My First Real Business Venture and the Oil Embargo That Swamped It

ALTHOUGH I HAD AN INCREDIBLE experience working for McKinsey, I learned that, for me, advising others was just not the same as taking full responsibility for running things. Toward the end of my time with McKinsey, I began to be on the lookout for new opportunities. One such opportunity arrived unexpectedly, as opportunities often do, in 1970 when I flew down to Hilton Head Island off the coast of South Carolina, at the invitation of my close friend Jim Light. Prior to our travels around the world on the Corning Fellowship, Jim and I had already been friends, having originally met at a wedding in my hometown of Kingsport, Tennessee, and later sharing an apartment together in Corning, New York, the summer before we set out on our trip. We both eventually attended Harvard Business School, and after Harvard, Jim took a position working for Charles Fraser, the famous developer, at the Sea Pines Company in Hilton Head, South Carolina. Jim invited me down from New York to play tennis and, my new passion at the time, golf.

Charles, with Jim's help, was still in the early stages of developing his 5,000-acre tract of land on Hilton Head Island. A significant portion of the 25,000-acre island was bought in the 1940s and 1950s for its timber value by his father, Joe Fraser, and his partners. It had previously been a bird-shooting plantation. In 1950, there were approximately 500 people, mostly farmers and oyster workers selling their wares in Savannah or nearby Bluffton, living on Hilton Head Island. Five years later, Charles, just out of Yale Law School at the age of twenty-six, set about converting his family's 5,000 acres of beaches, pine trees, and great live oak forests into a planned community. Sea Pines Plantation, as he named the resort community, would go on to become the first of a series of resorts that would earn him the reputation as a visionary in the field of community development. And quite rightly, Charles Fraser is credited with changing the land-use model of resort communities; he believed in low density, highly amenitized, tightly controlled development, and in utilizing restrictive covenants, setting architectural controls, and always committing a major portion of land to nature preserves, Charles created special communities.

With his considerable intellect, Charles learned a lot about nature, and this influenced his decision about which parcel of land to select when his family was given first choice once the land had been partitioned. Most people felt that the high bluff on the north end of the island, closest to the mainland, was the prime spot. But Charles knew that in the Northern Hemisphere, the littoral drift always moves sand to the south, just as it always moves sand to the north in the Southern Hemisphere. He loved great beaches and, figuring for the long term, chose the V-shaped tip on the south end of Hilton Head where today one finds Harbour Town with its landmark red-and-white lighthouse; Harbour Town Golf Links, designed by Jack Nicklaus and Pete Dye; three other golf courses; 1,250 acres of conservation land; and wide, spectacular beaches. As well, there are villas and homes that now house more than 5,000 people.

Charles was constantly reading, and one rarely saw him without a book in his hand. He studied concepts and ideas, treatises on architecture, land-use planning, and restrictive covenants. He studied how people behaved, how they used their time, and what they seemed to value in terms of their lifestyle and habits. Through this process, he achieved an understanding of people's strong preferences and, as a result, made every project he did early on beach oriented. A man of boundless energy, he would frequently share what he had learned with everyone he met and was always the center of any conversation. Being with Charles was never routine or boring.

Much of Hilton Head was master planned by the time I visited Jim Light in 1970, but Charles already had his next project lined up, having recently bought from C. Brewer a Hawaiian sugar company, 2,400 acres on the southeast coast of Puerto Rico. He was having trouble finding someone to run the project, expressing to me during my visit that he feared people might be intimidated by Jim Light, who had a reputation for being charming, attractive, and incredibly bright. "Who would be afraid of Jim Light?" I asked sarcastically when I heard this. Charles took notice and said to me, "Well, if you're so smart, why don't you fly down with us and take a look?"

Palmas del Mar, as it was called, was stunningly beautiful. It was a sugar cane and coconut plantation running five miles along the southeast coast of Puerto Rico, spilling down from high ridgelines to pristine sands. The view from my office window in Manhattan was not like this. But as spectacular as it was, I could feel that it was the possibility of what lay before me that excited me most. I knew nothing about building a resort, but I absolutely loved a challenge. So when Charles offered me the job of heading up Palmas del Mar, I grabbed it.

In 1971, I moved south, and for the first year in my new role, I lived at Hilton Head. I worked closely with Charles and Jim, soaking up their experience in master planning large-scale communities. We built relationships with three different real estate investment trusts—REITS, as they were called. The Chase Manhattan REIT was the lead lender to Palmas del Mar, while Barnett Bank's REIT in Jacksonville, Florida, was the lender for Palmas Harbor, the resort's harbor village, and Citibank's REIT was the lender for Monte Sol, the tennis village project at Palmas.

During that year at Hilton Head, I met Lucy Scardino through Jim, and a romance ensued. She lived in nearby Savannah with her three amazing daughters—Katherine, Robbie, and Liza, ages seven, six, and four, respectively, at the time. On one of our dates, as I waited for Lucy to go out for dinner, Robbie asked me, "Michael, when are you going to marry our mommy? She is dating another man from Atlanta who we call 'the truck driver,' and we want her to marry *you*." Robbie and her sisters were irresistible, and my love for them grew as much as my relationship with Lucy did during that year. Not long afterward, I proposed.

Lucy and I were married in December 1971 and shortly thereafter moved to Puerto Rico. For the first year, we lived in the outskirts of San Juan, then made the move to Palmas del Mar with the three young girls. In my role, I was stretched in the beginning, and the learning curve was steep. Work intensified, and I believe it was most challenging for my family. Thankfully, Lucy was a highly capable and productive person; she started a Montessori school that still exists at Palmas today. The girls loved horseback riding, living on the beach, and learning Spanish.

In terms of the real estate development project, we knew that a local planner and architect was critical to our development. Esteban Padilla, or Steve, as he was called, had attended Harvard and was one of Puerto Rico's best-known architects. He became the mastermind of the Palmas concept. Steve had studied the social and architectural structure of small villages in Europe and loved the Mediterranean villages along the coasts of France and Spain. At one point, he took Charles, Jim, me, and our wives on a tour of the best of these port villages so we could experience them up close. Steve was especially taken with Port Grimaud, a French village just a few kilometers down the coast from St. Tropez where, in the early '60s, an architect named François Spoerry had created a beautiful community out of marshlands around a port. The area was dominated by an eleventh-century castle that Spoerry had partially restored. We were all quite taken with what we saw, and Spoerry, who died in 1999, became a design consultant for us at Palmas. His influence can still be seen in the four villages that we built.

Meanwhile, I continued to do a lot of learning. While we had hired some great people for our luxury resort project and found some talented contractors, architects, and engineers, progress was not as fast as we would have liked. We were in Puerto Rico, and the government bureaucracy there meant that it took a long time to get things approved. Even more challenging was the fact that we needed roads, water, sewer, and telephone service to build our luxury resort, but the nearest town to Palmas del Mar was Humacao, about seven miles away, and it was a sleepy little sugar cane center that didn't have much to offer. Although the phone company was privately owned, we had to rely on government promises for all the other necessary utilities. Local government officials would assure us that the utilities and other basics we needed would be extended down to Palmas in time for our opening, but as opening day approached, they always seemed to come up with some other excuse as to why another eighteen-month-or-more delay would be necessary. Frustration and stress levels for our team intensified, and I was the most stressed of all.

Costs continued to rise. What had originally begun as a modest investment in roads—we always knew we would have to pay for the infrastructure within Palmas—ended up with expenditure of a lot more capital than we had anticipated. Suddenly, we were paying for water, electricity, and sewer lines that extended off the property and the entire seven-mile distance to Humacao. The telephone company was slow to keep its promises as well. We were in danger of not having phone service when we opened the hotel and 400 condominiums and ended up having to build a telephone substation behind Palmas Harbor.

We experienced other complications as well. To meet the challenges we faced, we also constructed an enormous water tank on top of the highest hill in Palmas. This water tank became symbolic some time later when the independentistas, the liberal, left-leaning, anti-US political force in Puerto Rico, planted a bomb at the base of the tank. Fortunately, the independentistas were not very good at building bombs, and although their device blew, it did not do much damage. At another point, they left a second bomb at one of our electric substations, only fifty yards from where we lived, but that luckily did not go off.

However difficult it became, we never believed our task was impossible.

We may not have been universally loved in Puerto Rico, but we did have, by the time we got up and running with our hotel and golf course, 400 wonderful and loyal employees, virtually all of them, except for me and a few of our management personnel, Puerto Rican. We were also receiving tremendous market interest in the project. Though the island today has tragically lost population and is in dire financial straits as it faces the gargantuan task of recovering from Hurricane Maria, Americans were willing to invest at that time and did not view Puerto Rico negatively. Despite the rising costs we faced, by 1973, we were able to start selling lots and homes. And, amid much excitement, the initial launch was a great success.

By this time, we had gone into partnership with ProServ, a firm founded by Donald Dell, the first sports agent in professional tennis and a former US Davis Cup captain and player. Dell represented the Davis Cup team of Arthur Ashe, Stan Smith, Bob Lutz, Charlie Pasarell, and Marty Riessen, and we were looking for the right man to install as tennis director at Palmas del Mar. Dell had been an aggressive player and shrewd Davis Cup captain, and he brought both those qualities to the boardroom. I remember him arriving to a meeting one day with a shiny aluminum Head racket that had just hit the market and was revolutionizing the industry. "If we get this deal done, there will be a lot more of these," he said with a chuckle.

Dell had been attracted to Palmas del Mar because it seemed like a perfect fit for Charlie Pasarell, who had come from a prominent Puerto Rican family. Charlie was already a leading player on the pro circuit and was showing the kind of vision that would lead him, eventually, to create in California the Grand Champions Resort for the ATP Indian Wells tournament and construct the Indian Wells Tennis Garden and its 16,000-seat stadium a mile down the road from that. He ultimately sold this entire complex to Larry Ellison, who has continued to invest in creating a fantastic tennis community. There was no doubt that Pasarell was the right man for the job, but neither he nor anyone else had much control over what would soon be in store for Palmas del Mar.

I remember that around this time, Arthur Ashe came down to look at the resort, and I gave him a full day's briefing. In a pragmatic assessment that was so typical of Arthur, he told me, "This is either going to be the most spectacular resort in the world or a giant bust." Unhappily, his second prediction was correct.

Everything looked good for a while. We'd sold our first 400 lots and condos, and the proceeds from these sales went some way to paying off the $100 million we had borrowed from the REITS. The success of Sea Pines had made borrowing easy, and there looked to be a clear road ahead with Palmas Harbor and Pasarell's Monte Sol up and running.

We experienced an early success when *Sports Illustrated* chose Palmas as the site for one of its swimsuit issues. The cover story featured the spectacular red, orange, and yellow mosaic-tile-covered pool we'd built at the Sun Fun Hut, and adorned with stunning models in bikinis, Palmas seemed off to a roaring start.

We also gained a great deal of good publicity in January 1975 by staging the CBS Tennis Classic, which Dell helped us arrange. All of Dell's clients participated in the classic, as well as other top pros. The great Rod Laver ended up winning the title, beating Arthur Ashe in the men's final, and Billie Jean King won the women's tournament, beating Chris Evert in the women's final. It was an exciting event.

And about this time, a new addition to the Ainslie family arrived when, in June 1974, Michael Loren Ainslie, better known as Miguelito, was born at Presbyterian Hospital in San Juan. I will never forget returning late that night to Palmas and stopping at the bar of the Palmas Inn. Our dear friend and piano player Avo Uvezian had composed a beautiful song in tribute to young Michael, our new arrival. Avo went on to much bigger things, as he became a cigar maker and today graces the pages of *Cigar Aficionado* with his white linen suit, straw hat, and cigar from his now famous line of AVO cigars.

I had much to be grateful for in work and in life during this period. And though our team had faced many initial obstacles with Palmas del Mar, I was proud of what we'd achieved and I was looking forward to continued success. We'd planned, prepared, and paved the way for a solid future at our resort. What could go wrong?

The 1973–74 oil embargo was what went wrong. Suddenly, in August 1974, you had trouble buying gas in the United States, and there were lines for miles at gas stations. Because of the embargo, imposed by members of the Organization of Petroleum Exporting Countries (OPEC) against the United States for its perceived support of Israel during the 1973 Arab–Israeli War, the United States had essentially run out of gas. Panic set in, credit dried up, and people tried frantically to get out of paying any superfluous expense to maintain their financial survival, like a beautiful second home in the Caribbean. Arthur Burns, the Federal Reserve chairman at the time, took interest rates to previously unknown levels of 12% and 13%, and for Palmas del Mar, our floating-rate REIT loans at 3% and 4% over prime became toxic.

The second thing that went wrong was our construction company. Our first big condominium, the Beach Village, was being constructed by IBEC Bland, one of Nelson Rockefeller's companies that built housing all over Latin America. While we quickly sold the first seventy-two villas, a buyer was able to cancel a purchase contract in Puerto Rico if the unit was not delivered in eighteen months. Sadly, IBEC Bland failed to deliver, and the $40 million of planned cash flow from these units never materialized.

Palmas del Mar was the most serious of Charles Fraser's problems but not his only one. His highly praised developments at Sea Pines, Amelia Island, Big Canoe in Atlanta, Charlotte's Riverhills, and Brandermill outside Richmond, Virginia, were also hit hard. Charles had personally taken on the task of finding a really big financial partner, but the oil crisis was having a devastating effect on the world economy and there was only so much he could do. We talked to Amoco, but they demurred. We brought in the great wheeler-dealer Adnan Khashoggi, who was reputedly worth $4 billion at the time and quite notorious, to help us out, but he said no. And we talked to the Kuwait Investment Company, which eventually bought Kiawah Island and lured Sea Pines to plan and develop it. But we were still sitting on a huge amount of borrowed money as the global recession set in during 1974–75, and we simply could not repay our loans.

Throughout 1974, Terry Golden, who was my chief financial officer, and I, Ron Terwilliger, and others up at Hilton Head were desperately trying to come up with a solution—winding down, cutting every cost we could. But in early 1975, it became clear that we were swimming against a tide that would eventually engulf us. We entered an informal bankruptcy process known as "deed in lieu" in which we simply gave the deeds to our REIT lenders instead of going through a more lengthy and costly bankruptcy. Some felt that we were being too friendly, that we should have fought them—certainly Charles Fraser could say to his lenders that his properties were more valuable *with* him than without him. There was one Philadelphia lawyer who said to us at the time, "Fight the sons of bitches. Don't give in to them so easily."

That was above my level in terms of what was being discussed and negotiated. By the middle of that year, it became clear to me that we did not have the right financial structure, and I needed to move on. I had worked incredibly hard for five years with an amazing team, and I was extremely upset to have to leave the people I had recruited to build what we felt would become a phenomenal community. But of paramount importance to me was my family. I had a wife and four kids, and I needed to get a job where I could support them.

With the word out that I was looking for a new role, I was approached by my old friend and headhunter Jacques Nordeman, the founder of Nordeman Grimm, a small but well-respected headhunting firm. Not long afterward, I was offered a good position as chief operating officer of N-ReN, a family-owned fertilizer company in Cincinnati. I remember feeling that I needed to reach for security. The resort real estate world had become too volatile a business for me at that time, and with a family, I couldn't put up with the swings and roundabouts of businesses that could go from such a giant upside to such an enormous downside. It had been an exhilarating time initially, but in the end, I knew I had also learned some hard lessons about the dangers of leaving a company exposed financially through overborrowing. Because of these experiences, I was able to avoid the same mistakes later at Sotheby's. If I had never been through a major market correction like that, it would have been difficult for me to anticipate the dangers.

In spite of the financial difficulties of these times, Charles Fraser remained positive and never cast blame. I think it would have been easy for him to have become negative and attack people, but I never saw that in him. Even when it came time for me to depart, we stayed friends, and I continued to see him and his wife during return trips to Hilton Head. Also, our daughters were of the same age and good friends, so we kept in touch that way.

I learned from Charles to create quality and to do things the right way. He was committed to that. He was all about community. And he was oriented toward the entire family and how each person would spend his or her leisure time. I saw the way he changed the face of resort development in America, as well as globally. He took a comprehensive approach, with everything planned and included from day one, and built communities that would work long term for everyone, with well-thought-out amenities and protective covenants. He was clearly less concerned about short-term profit than creating something that had lasting value. I think, as one looks back today at Sea Pines, Hilton Head Plantation, Amelia, and Kiawah, one can see the results of Fraser's genius.

When we were in the midst of the Palmas del Mar financial crisis, my wife, Lucy, needlepointed a plaque for Charles's office wall. It depicted an alligator with a quote reading, "When you are up to your ass in alligators, it is difficult to remember your initial objective was to drain the swamp." I remember Lucy giving it to Charles. He loved it.

I'm thankful for the legacy Charles left and the invaluable life lessons he gave me through Palmas del Mar that helped me so much in avoiding the pitfalls that lay ahead. Ours was a lifelong friendship. From Charles I learned the real measure of a man is in the beliefs and values he stands for, not his net worth.

Refocusing the National Trust

9

My Path to Public Service

LIFE IS FULL OF INTERESTING turns that can lead you in directions you never knew you'd go. If you are open to new opportunities, focused on doing things of value, and observant of those around you, sometimes you wind up exactly where you were meant to be. I served as president and CEO of the National Trust for Historic Preservation from 1980 to 1984. My path to this position came about through one of these unexpected turns in life. It began during my five years in Cincinnati while I was running N-ReN, the nitrogen fertilizer and energy company I took on after leaving Palmas del Mar.

Cincinnati, the sixth-largest city in America in 1850, was filled with wonderful architecture from that period. Looking around for something to fill our spare time, Lucy and I started buying old buildings and renovating them. She had spent years heavily involved in preservation while living in Savannah, and I brought my real estate experience from Palmas. We bought and restored about fifteen buildings, and during that period we became friendly with Carl Westmoreland, a trustee of the National Trust for Historic Preservation. Carl had been restoring homes and apartments in his low-income neighborhood of Mount Auburn, working hard to create affordable housing for people. He and I became good friends, and I found myself becoming more involved in his projects.

Because of the contacts I had made through Carl, the National Trust and its chairman Carlisle Humelsine came calling. They were looking for a new president with new ideas who had the courage to broaden the mission of the National Trust. Although I had always wanted to work in some form of public service, I recognized the fact that I had four kids and an expensive wife to think about, so I rejected their initial courtship. But Carlisle improved the offer for the National Trust presidency by leasing for us a beautiful Victorian townhouse in Georgetown. It was an incredible opportunity, so Lucy and I decided to move our family to Washington.

Bringing some of our own period furniture from Cincinnati, we were soon enjoying the stimulating life of the nation's capital. I found myself in a high-profile position in which I was tasked with leading a nonpolitical, nonpartisan, nonprofit organization. I loved the challenge, not just for the sake of heading up an important organization but also for having the opportunity to change it. My idea of leadership was then, as it is now, to bring in new ideas and change things for the better. I'd learned that even if I ran into stiff opposition on occasion, throwing light on an issue and offering concrete, doable suggestions usually lowered the barriers. And my experience in leading the National Trust in the early '80s was no different.

Before I took over, the National Trust had shown little interest in doing anything for run-down historic buildings in low-income neighborhoods, and this work had been left to neighborhood activists like Carl Westmoreland and a remarkable woman I met named Joan Maynard. Through their efforts, I quickly recognized the importance of identifying buildings of historic value that were located in lower-income inner-city historic districts and the importance of doing something to better these communities. To me, the fact that 60% of historic districts were low income was compelling reason enough for the National Trust to get involved.

Joan Maynard, a former art director at McGraw-Hill, had grown up in Brooklyn. She no doubt learned some of her speaking skills from her father, John Cooper, who was a ventriloquist. Joan, however, never left you in any doubt that she was speaking from her own mouth, and in 1968, she founded the Society for the Preservation of Weeksville, a run-down but historic section of Bedford-Stuyvesant. There had been little interaction with the National Trust up to that point, but after Joan received federal funding to restore four mid-nineteenth-century buildings on Hunterfly Road, she was invited to join the National Trust's board. She and I worked closely for several years, and I was grateful to learn from this special lady. Though she passed away in 2006, she left an amazing legacy, having dedicated much of her life to trying to improve conditions in black neighborhoods, inspired, as she said, by her mother's tales of inequality growing up in Granada. From her, I learned that combining education with preservation creates far more community support than simply asking people to save buildings. Joan made her neighborhood proud of its history.

The National Trust was responsible for preserving major homes and buildings throughout the country, and although we were only in charge of buildings as opposed to thousands of acres of countryside, as is the case in Britain, the challenge was still monumental. It is a sad fact of life that in America, it is cheaper to tear down a building and start again than to restore it. As president of the National Trust, I found that we were always in need of funding, and this often proved difficult to find.

My early days at the National Trust happened to coincide with the election of Ronald Reagan, which did not necessarily augur well for an organization like ours. Nevertheless, we believed in our work and, during that time, thought it best to bite the bullet, approaching Reagan's new secretary of the interior, James Watt, to ask for assistance. I remember taking my board chairman Alan Boyd, a former secretary of transportation and then CEO of Amtrak, along to see Watt. But we ran into a stone wall. "Preservation is a liberal East Coast establishment phenomenon, and this administration is not going to have anything to do with it!" was the insulting admonishment we received from Watt. That might have seemed like a dead end as far as the Reagan administration was concerned, but we knew it was important not to let Secretary Watt have the last word. We decided we should take a different tack.

President Reagan, at the time, was preparing to pass a major tax reform bill in 1981. This bill would reduce tax rates and cut big government in a major way. But the chairman of the House Ways and Means Committee, one of the most powerful committees on Capitol Hill, happened to be a Democrat named Dan Rostenkowski, a larger-than-life figure who fought his way out of Chicago politics to establish himself as a force in Washington. When, as head of the National Trust, I approached him to see if he might be able to help us on tax matters, I knew he would be compelled if there was a way to benefit his Chicago district. We did a little clandestine inspection work in his home district in Chicago, counting the buildings in his district that were in various states of disrepair. Though there were a lot of them, most could not be classified as historic. Nevertheless, we knew that if we could write a provision to be inserted into the new tax law that would reduce the cost of renovation of all types of buildings, his district would reap enormous benefits, particularly if we could target non-historic thirty- and forty-year-old buildings.

After a certain amount of politicking, Rostenkowski got the message, realizing how beneficial this could be for his constituents. John Salmon, who was his chief of staff, and I crafted the wording for a set of tax incentives that saw historic buildings receive a 25% tax credit for certified rehabilitation; non-historic buildings that were forty years old would get a 20% credit, and thirty-year-old buildings a 15% tax credit on renovations. These tax credits were an incredible boost to preservation and radically changed the economics of rehabilitating from difficult to very positive. Without question, the 1981 Historic Tax Credits were a game changer for the national preservation movement. The historic building tax credits still exist today but have been reduced to 20%. Since that time, more than 42,000 historic buildings have seen nearly $90 billion of investment.[1] This was the biggest public policy change toward historic preservation our country has ever seen.

The tax credits took the National Trust way beyond its concentration on "white glove" preservation, as house museums and restored homes of great figures in American history were called. But I also knew there was much that could be done to improve the lot of ordinary people by upgrading whole neighborhoods. I discovered a pilot program, active in only three small towns, called the Main Street program. This program was working to revitalize small towns of under 50,000 people. The National Trust model utilized a coalition of local banks for loan funds, colleges and universities for design support, and a strong project manager in each town to mobilize the merchants with parking strategies, downtown festivals, and shared marketing, with identical hours of operation. Clearly, this program had national potential, but how to roll it out was the question.

After some brainstorming sessions, we concluded that governors were the key. We asked for proposals and were amazed that thirty-nine states submitted proposals to be selected as one of the six initial states to be included in the national Main Street program. Texas, North Carolina, Massachusetts, Colorado, Georgia, and Pennsylvania were selected as the first states to launch the Main Street program, and as the years went by, Main Street had such success that the National Trust spun it out into a new nonprofit, Main Street America, in 2015.

Today, more than 284,000 buildings have been rehabilitated with nearly $79 billion invested in 1,600 communities.[2] The program grew to include not only small towns but also commercial districts in larger cities. Clearly, the National Trust has had an impact way beyond its early focus on house museums.

A young, practical visionary named Mary Means created and crafted the Main Street program, aided by a team of passionate advocates. She found a way to link preservation with economic revitalization, and the result has been rebirth for hundreds of small towns. In 2019, the American Planning Association gave her much-deserved recognition, naming her a National Planning Pioneer.

Another successful new initiative of the National Trust during my tenure was the Inner Cities Ventures Fund, which supported community organizations creating affordable housing in low-income historic districts.

This program took a page from Carl Westmoreland's playbook, and I was proud of the positive effect we made in cities around the United States.

As often happens in life, things don't always go smoothly, and we need to think quickly and attempt to bring our best to a situation. The National Trust received a $1 million donation from Sohio, an oil company, to support our work in inner-city neighborhoods in Ohio. As president of the National Trust, I was asked to travel to Columbus to accept the check from the company. Unhappily, my arrival coincided with Sohio imploding its thirty-story historic headquarters building downtown, and the timing made for a juicy news story for media outlets. The press was all over me that day, wanting to know how this could be consistent with the National Trust's policy of preserving, rather than destroying, historic buildings. I was flabbergasted at the events myself. There was no easy answer, but I tried to make light of it by saying that it would not be too bad if we got a check for a million bucks every time a building was torn down.

As we broadened the scope of the National Trust, there were obstacles we couldn't always foresee. In the work of historic preservation, we discovered that although local merchants were active in the refurbishment of their buildings, the process was often an uphill struggle for them. In reality, there was a serious shortage of architects who knew how to properly restore buildings. So the National Trust took on the charge of running courses to teach architects how to do restoration. I think it's a worthwhile lesson in life to remember that one needs to think of the secondary requirements of a new program, which often are the cause of failure or slow progress.

My job experience at the National Trust enriched me. It also gave me the ability to apply what I'd learned from the first few years of my career. My nose for trouble would continue to bring me into unusual, sometimes uncomfortable, but always interesting situations. I tried to embrace them and use them to produce positive change. In many ways, these years made me a better, stronger, and more entrepreneurial leader.

10

Partner Building

I **TREASURED MY TIME WITH THE** National Trust. I like to think I was effective in my position as president, not only doing work that was meaningful and worthwhile in terms of historic preservation but also leading the trust to take a more active role in community building in a way it had never embraced before. Because we were, in many ways, operating in unchartered territory, we faced new challenges. But those years also positioned the National Trust for growth and allowed me to meet some amazing people. The National Trust gave me a unique platform for doing something beneficial for others.

...

WHEN I ARRIVED AT the National Trust in early 1980, I learned that Nelson Rockefeller, upon his sudden and untimely death in January 1979, had left to the National Trust his one-fourth interest in a section of Pocantico Hills, where the family estate is located in Westchester County. This came as a surprise to the public but also to his brothers who suddenly found themselves with a public charity as a partner in a very private family retreat.

Further, I found that the National Trust had its general counsel dealing with the Rockefeller family and antagonizing them at every turn. He retired shortly thereafter, and I personally took on the Rockefeller relationship, having almost daily contact with David Rockefeller and his Milbank Tweed lawyer Donal O'Brien, a talented man with whom I built a wonderful working relationship.

We ultimately arrived at an agreement for Laurance and David Rockefeller to leave their shares of Pocantico to the National Trust upon their deaths. A $16 million endowment was established as a gift from the Rockefeller Brothers Fund and began growing so it could provide for the long-term care of the family estate when the trust finally took over. This complex agreement was consummated in December 1983. Little did we suspect that David Rockefeller would live another thirty-four years, passing away in 2017 at 101 years of age.

Rockefeller gift of eighty-six acres of Pocantico Hills to the National Trust, December 1983. Michael Ainslie; Blanchette Hooker Rockefeller, widow of John D. Rockefeller III; New York governor Mario Cuomo; David Rockefeller; and Happy Rockefeller, widow of Nelson Rockefeller.

30 Rockefeller Plaza
New York, N.Y. 10112

Room 5600   247-3700

#2

January 10, 1984

Dear Michael:

    Enclosed are some photographs which were taken at the
Pocantico press conference. I thought you might like to have
them as a momento of that happy occasion.

    I am very sorry that I cannot be with you today for your
tour of Kykuit, but know that Bob Snyder will see that everything
goes smoothly.

    With kind regards,

                              Sincerely,

                              David Rockefeller

Mr. Michael L. Ainslie
President
National Trust for Historic Preservation
1785 Massachusetts Avenue NW
Washington, DC 20036

Letter from David Rockefeller, January 1984.

However, the plan to let the Rockefeller family continue to have exclusive use of Pocantico through the life of all the brothers was aborted by Robert Bass, who followed Alan Boyd as chairman of the National Trust. Bass took over shortly after my departure to Sotheby's. He felt the public should have access to Pocantico sooner than our agreement called for, so he and David Rockefeller, somewhat painfully, restructured the agreement to provide public access during the summer months (when the Rockefellers were primarily in Maine).[1] Given the surprising length of David's life, this restructuring turned out to be a positive improvement that allowed much earlier public access.

...

THOUGH MY EFFORTS WITH the National Trust didn't necessarily always yield the results I hoped for, they did enable me to still advocate for and have a voice in important programs and initiatives. On March 30, 1981, First Lady Nancy Reagan and Second Lady Barbara Bush came to the historic Georgetown townhouse where I lived with Lucy and our four children. We had invited them as lunch guests on that Monday because I was trying to persuade the First Lady to take an active role in the national Main Street program, the highly successful program that was revitalizing small towns across America. Up until that point, Mrs. Reagan had gained a reputation for doing little other than worry about which china to choose for White House dinners. We felt that with her becoming the patron of the national Main Street program, she would be provided with an ideal opportunity to be linked to a cause that cut across partisan lines.

At first, her staff said she would not be available but eventually agreed to have her stop by for a few minutes. She stayed for more than two hours through a long luncheon with us, though in the end, sadly, she did not agree to become involved as our principal spokesperson for the program.

In contrast, Barbara Bush was rather more active on all fronts, as she proved when she later became the First Lady. We enjoyed seeing a little of how her mind worked on the day she came for lunch. Some days before our luncheon, Mrs. Bush had been quoted in *The Washington Post* as stating that, although everyone thought the vice president's family lived in luxury in the beautiful Naval Observatory, the furniture left something to be desired. "I hope people will give the house furniture donations. We especially need some chests," she said in the article.[2] On hearing this, Lucy had the idea of making a permanent loan of an elegant antique Victorian chest, an item from the National Trust's furniture inventory, to the vice president's home. On the day of the luncheon, the chest was sitting behind the front door to our residence, and after Mrs. Reagan departed the luncheon, we made the presentation to Mrs. Bush. She appeared delighted and said she would take a photograph to show us the old crate when she got home.

We did not realize what a fateful day it was. Minutes after Nancy Reagan left, right before three o'clock, the caterer rushed out of our kitchen, shouting what he had just heard on the television: "President Reagan's been shot!" It was a dramatic moment for the whole country but, for us, sobering in a much different way. At that moment in time, no one in our home knew if the president would live. And Barbara Bush, with her husband as vice president, was teetering on the edge of history as she suddenly faced the possibility of becoming First Lady at any moment.

She needed to depart, of course, and as we all know, President Reagan survived. But Lucy and I noted that though Mrs. Bush had every reason to be distracted with President Reagan's condition and the prospect that her husband might become president, remarkably, she followed up on her conversation with us. The next day, along with a nice thank-you note for the lunch, we received a Polaroid photograph of the orange crate she'd told us about, an old campaign chest with the pulls hanging off, half detached. Thankfully, George Bush did not become president through a tragedy on that Monday, but the National Trust was glad to have the opportunity to at least give him a more appropriate place to keep his shirts.

Day of the shooting of President Reagan, March 30, 1981. Michael Ainslie and Lucy Scardino Ainslie making a presentation to Barbara Bush of a Victorian chest of drawers so that Vice President George Bush could keep his shirts in something other than an "orange crate." Photo credit: Carleton Knight III for the National Trust for Historic Preservation.

Michael Ainslie speaking to Nancy Reagan, Alan Boyd (the National Trust chair), and other guests at the luncheon, March 1981. Photo credit: Carleton Knight III for the National Trust for Historic Preservation.

...

IN MY ROLE WITH the National Trust, traveling out of town to make speeches on preservation at meetings and conferences became a way of life, and during a typical month, I would probably make four or five major speeches all over the country. Often, I found the local preservationists in conflict with their mayor, but at every turn, I presented myself as a pragmatist who did not want to stand in the way of progress just for the sake of fighting over a building. I wanted to be part of the solution to the never-ending argument over what to save and what to tear down. I wanted to stop the fighting, but it took a lot of negotiating, backed by some innovative ideas.

Mayors, I quickly learned, wanted peace, not war. In city after city, I could see the potential for bringing parties together, often after some study of the conflict. I convinced the National Trust board to let me make grants of up to $25,000 to a city or leading local organization if, in turn, the mayor or local officials would match the grant; through this partnership, the National Trust would then use the funds to launch a zoning or preservation study to try to solve the issue. We called this program the Critical Issues Fund, but my staff unofficially referred to it as "Michael's walking-around money."

On one occasion, I went to Salt Lake City where the Mormon Church was in a huge battle with the Utah Trust for Historic Preservation over Eagle Gate, an apartment building downtown that the Mormon Church owned and wanted to tear down. I asked for a meeting with the Mormon Church Council of Elders and was amazed when they agreed to meet with me.

On my arrival at the temple, I was ushered into a remarkable 200-foot-long marble entry hall, completely white except for a woven purple carpet. I knew that five wise men of the Mormon Church were waiting for me, but as I entered the inner sanctum, I paused, wondering how I should proceed in that moment. Though I hadn't necessarily expected any particular kind of welcome, the scene before me was surprising. The men I was to meet with were hunched down, immobile, and appeared to be, well, almost dead. Quickly, I launched into my little speech to see if I could get some sort of reaction. "You are facing a real battle with the preservation movement in your community," I told them. "But let me propose a solution. We'll give you a $25,000 grant. If you will match that grant, we will conduct an inventory of your downtown and jointly be able to decide which buildings are truly historic and which are just old and don't need to be preserved."

A long silence followed. They huddled and whispered to one another. Then, to my surprise, they said, "We accept your offer." It was a great win on many fronts, and there was progress and peace in Salt Lake City. We found that the Critical Issues Fund, part of my plan to resolve local disputes, enabled us to win a lot of preservation battles and a lot of new friends.

...

ON ONE OCCASION, THE National Trust took another tack and, instead of trying to restore buildings, campaigned to prevent the altering of an existing one—and a famous one at that. In 1982, Tip O'Neill was in his prime. He was, perhaps, the most powerful and dominant Speaker of the House that Congress had ever known. With his mane of white hair, a figure as large as his personality, and his fierce loyalty to the Democratic politics of his native Boston, O'Neill was as Irish as his name. O'Neill liked, aside from a glass of whiskey, his food and was reported to have been appalled when he was once served a muffin and coffee instead of bacon and eggs at a White House breakfast. "But Mr. President, we did win!" he is reported to have grumbled to President Carter.

With visions of culinary delight in his mind, O'Neill came up with a plan to extend the US Capitol Building facing the National Mall. His plan called for filling in the two deep recesses in the façade of the Capitol, thereby creating two new restaurants. Given that it would have drastically changed an icon called "the most recognizable building in the free

world" by Senator Patrick Moynihan at our rally, we, at the National
Trust, decided the plan was an abomination and went to work to stop it
in its tracks.

We organized a big "Save the Capitol" rally on the steps of the
West Front of the Capitol and targeted the media so successfully that
300 newspapers across the country wrote editorials strongly opposing
O'Neill's plan. All this had such an effect that, in a rare roll call vote in
the House, 350 members voted against Speaker O'Neill and his atro-
cious plan. It wasn't easy to defeat O'Neill, and looking back, I'm enormously proud of that achievement.

Michael Ainslie, president of the National Trust for Historic Preservation,
leading the "Save the Capitol" rally, October 1982.

...

AT ANOTHER POINT IN my years with the National Trust, I oversaw an attempt to find a compromise in a feud that broke out between the Reverend Thomas Bowers, rector of St. Bartholomew's Church (St. Bart's), a national landmark on the corner of Park Avenue and East Fiftieth Street in Manhattan, and the New York Landmarks Conservancy. Bowers, whose congregation had shrunk dramatically, was crying poverty and wanted to sell the church's community hall to a British developer that was willing to pay $100 million to build a huge tower in its place. But just like the New York Racquet Club across the street and St Patrick's Cathedral on Fifth Avenue, St. Bart's had air rights above its building that were probably worth millions. The air rights would have this value only if they could be sold to the developer of an adjacent property.

Jacqueline Kennedy and other New York City notables joined in the outcry against a tower being built that would loom over St. Bart's. Opponents of the sale were horrified when Bowers's planner came up with a proposal to build a cantilevered building covering a corner of the church and rising fifty stories above.

Realizing that this dispute would do nothing other than make lawyers rich, I got involved and suggested we explore an expanded use of TDRs, or transfer of development rights, which allowed an environmentally protected property to sell its air rights to adjacent sites. Unfortunately, all the adjacent sites were already fully developed and unable to utilize the St. Bart's air rights; their value, as a result, was seriously depreciated. Knowing a bit about New York politics, I went to work with my old friend Jay Kriegel and the mayor's office to gain their support for extending the transfer options to more distant sites for a limited number of buildings that had national landmark designation. This of course included St. Bart's.

In spite of our efforts, the Reverend Bowers was not a man interested in compromise. Although a modified TDR solution would have brought peace and millions of dollars to his church, he pushed ahead with his development scheme in hopes of making even more. Sadly, the reverend's greed led him to get nothing. He instead received a severe rebuff when his plans and arguments were put before the New York Landmarks Preservation Commission.

Scarcely a single aspect of the church's case withstood scrutiny, per the commission. In a devastating piece in the *New York Post* on February 26, 1986, reporter Guy Hawtin wrote, "The commissioners made it clear that they believe that senior officials of the controversial Park Avenue Episcopal church deliberately set out to bamboozle and mislead them. Commissioner Anthony Tung . . . summed it all up . . . 'This is such a painful case,' he said. 'To look at an application so fraught with questionable practices and numbers . . . was frankly dismaying.'"[3] The words were, if anything, an understatement.

In 1994, the Reverend William MacDonald Tully took over from Bowers and got St. Bart's back on its feet. Today, it is a strong church that provides much-needed shelter for the city's homeless on cold winter nights.

That Reverend Bowers had refused to accept a compromise in this high-profile case was frustrating, but at least I had shown that the National Trust could inject itself into disputes of this nature to find a solution. In my years as president, I'm glad that I managed to lead the trust into a different and less rigid place. I worked then to communicate a message of partnership and collaboration. And I still believe in that model now.

· · ·

I LOVED MY YEARS at the National Trust, but sadly, my marriage to Lucy ended in divorce in 1983, and I needed to move on from that stage of my career. Ours was an exciting but always challenging marriage, and the later years were difficult for both of us.

I know I did not initially make it easy, moving our family to Puerto Rico in the early years where many problems faced us in my work. Though

Lucy coped well there, starting a school and being a great mother to our four children, I wish my role had demanded less of our family.

Ultimately, our preservation involvement proved too much. When I was hired to become president of the National Trust, Lucy wanted to have a major role, since she, in many ways, knew more about historic preservation than I did. She'd spent many of her earlier years involved with the Historic Savannah Foundation and the Victorian Society of America, but when she eventually began telling staff at the National Trust what to do, it did not work. Only one of us could be the boss, so we grew apart, and after long efforts at counseling, we decided to go our separate ways. She's an incredibly bright person, and I learned much from her.[4] We remain civil, share four children and lots of grandkids, and have each gone on to happy lives with new partners.

. . .

TOWARD THE END OF my time with the National Trust, at a Harvard Business School meeting on entrepreneurship, I went for a run along the Charles River with my old friend Jacques Nordeman, the headhunter who had introduced me to my former job in Cincinnati. I told Jacques that I needed a new job since I now had two households to support, mine and Lucy's. Because the Cincinnati job had not turned out as he and I had originally hoped, I told him that he "owed me one." Little did I know that only a few months later, Al Taubman, a wealthy shopping mall magnate and investor, would buy Sotheby's and hire Nordeman to find him a new CEO.

Modernizing Sotheby's

11

The Changing of an Institution

OTHEBY'S HAS A LONG-STANDING REPUTATION of being one of the world's largest and most venerable brokers of jewelry, fine art and collectibles, and luxury real estate. When I was approached to take over as its CEO in 1984, it would have been impossible for me to envisage this 240-year-old British institution becoming enveloped in any kind of scandal, let alone the embarrassing price-fixing scandal with which it would later be associated. This was a notorious episode involving collusion between Sotheby's and Christie's, the other major auction house, and it created damaging ripple effects that rocked the art world to its core. I loved my years with Sotheby's, grieved when I learned of this scandal, and share my story with you, not only to offer an inside view of the events that transpired but also to allow you to see beyond the scandal to a truly great institution I'm proud to have brought into the modern era.

That is not to say Sotheby's was a perfectly run company at the time that I joined it. It was a mess as far as management and leadership were concerned. But that was the motivating factor for me when I agreed to leave my job with the National Trust in Washington, DC, and move to New York. To me, Sotheby's presented a challenge—just the sort of challenge I was looking for—and I wanted to bring a positive change to an old establishment.

Jacques Nordeman, the headhunter and my former Harvard Business

School friend, introduced me to Al Taubman in the fall of 1983, but during our first meeting, the robust discussion Taubman and I had about the future of Sotheby's came to nothing. Taubman offered me the top job at Sotheby's International Realty, but that didn't interest me. I returned to Washington, not expecting anything more to come of our conversation, especially since Nordeman had let me know that Taubman was looking for a gray-haired European to become the top man at Sotheby's, and as a forty-year-old southerner with a full head of brown hair, I didn't exactly seem to fit the bill. But after four or five months, it became clear that there was no gray-haired European in sight. Sotheby's had ceased being a publicly traded stock on the London exchange and had become a private company that year, but the man Taubman had put in place as an interim CEO, David Ward, a partner in his auditing firm, was getting nowhere and appeared to be a fish out of water in that role. Everyone involved, including Taubman, was growing impatient, so I got another phone call.

This time, after another day spent talking with Taubman about the big changes needed at Sotheby's, the message was more to my liking. "You're my guy," Taubman said. "Come and run Sotheby's."

When Al Taubman purchased Sotheby's for $130 million, he put up $40 million for his 60% of the company, with his partners Max Fisher, Les Wexner, Henry Ford, Bill Pitt, Milton Petrie, Earl Smith, and other investors putting in $25 million for the other 40% of stock. They also borrowed $65 million from Chase Manhattan Bank to fund the balance of the acquisition.[1] In my decade as CEO, Taubman's $40 million initial investment produced more than $600 million in dividends and stock value. This was a 31% compound annual return for those ten years. Al Taubman owned a company that was worth ten times what it was when he bought it, which, in my view, wasn't a bad investment.

But this rise in the company's fortunes did not happen by chance. As I mentioned, given the state the company was in when I arrived, major changes were required to turn it into a cohesive and profitable organization.

That we managed to bring the changes about made those early years at Sotheby's extremely satisfying.

...

WHEN I JOINED SOTHEBY'S, I was full of trepidation because of my limited art knowledge. It did not take me long to realize that the company's challenges did not lie in the realm of art expertise, which it had in great depth. It needed saving in many other ways. Held in a vise by age-old traditions, Sotheby's was in need of major changes in its business practices to succeed in the increasingly competitive art marketplace. I saw the potential but was troubled by the fact that the company, founded in 1744, still behaved as if it were in the eighteenth century.

The company's biggest problem lay in the marketplace. We were selling to the wrong customer. Most of our auction sales went to art dealers, not private collectors. Taubman, as a collector, realized this and saw it as a major opportunity. I quickly grasped this as I saw repeated examples of practices that made life easy for our experts but that ignored the private client. It took much more work to educate and excite a private client than to have a dealer pay wholesale and need no help in learning about the work of art. It was clear to me that our big competitor was not Christie's but the art dealer.

To make things even more complicated, Sotheby's, I could see, was a house divided. There was the London office, full of cobwebs, both literal and attitudinal, hidebound in the British way of doing things. And then there was New York, where the company was still tied to the name Sotheby Parke-Bernet, following the 1967 merger with Parke-Bernet, the old New York auction house. New York did not like London, or, more specifically, John Marion, chairman of Sotheby Parke-Bernet in New York, could not stand the London management. In particular, Marion, of Irish heritage, clashed with the global CEO Graham Llewellyn, whose Welsh blood was seen to boil when two American entrepreneurs, Marshall Cogan and Stephen Swid, had previously moved to buy the company before Al Taubman stepped in and outbid them. According to a report in *The Washington Post*, Llewellyn had threatened to blow his brains out if Cogan and Swid succeeded.[2] Marion was, for decades, the most talented and effective auctioneer around, so he had a sound basis for his criticism.

Evidently, Taubman's successful intervention diverted the need for Llewellyn to pull the trigger, but when I arrived on the scene, it was obvious that animosity was running high between the stuffy British establishment and those Colonials across the Atlantic. When I joined, the volume of auction sales was roughly equal between the New York and London offices, but I saw that New York and London often competed against each other for consignments of major painting collections.

To complicate things further, the computers in the two offices couldn't speak to each other. New York used IBM, while London had a contract with Burroughs, which was, ironically, a Detroit-based company. After an exhaustive review, we chose IBM and set about building a worldwide client database. Although it turned out to be a two-year project and cost Sotheby's $10 million, I knew this was a crucial step in dragging the place into the modern age.

In the early years, nothing seemed more antiquated to me than our famous London headquarters on Bond Street. It was a maze of buildings leading through to Conduit Street, tied together over the centuries on slanting, uneven floors with endless up-and-down staircases. With Taubman leading the way, we undertook a complete reconfiguring of the thirteen buildings that made up Sotheby's London. We spent £10 million on this renovation, and we did it with careful attention to the traditional British style and architecture that gave the Bond Street premises their charm. Taubman was at his best on a project like this, using his architectural and spatial brilliance to redesign Sotheby's London.

I ran into the full brunt of British stubbornness when, as part of the planning for the renovations, I mentioned air-conditioning. Why didn't we have it? "Oh, because we don't work in the summer, and it doesn't get hot that often anyway," was the answer. My response to this was firm. From that moment on, we would be working in the summer, and there would be air-conditioning.

I was also met with the same looks of horror and disdain when I banned smoking at all London meetings. In Europe in the '80s, a majority of people smoked (even smoking on planes was the norm). My ban was highly unpopular at first, but, in fact, people came around quite quickly and, after a few weeks, most of our people were agreeing with me, which was a good thing because in me they had a CEO who was allergic to cigarette smoke.

Changes were needed in New York, too, and some of them were quite visible. Considerably more contentious to the company was the decision I made to eliminate the Parke-Bernet name. This was especially a highly unpopular move in New York, where I ran into a lot of opposition. But I stuck to the argument that the name Sotheby's needed to be turned into a global brand and that clients in New York, Paris, Hong Kong, and Tokyo did not need to be confused by the company using different names at their two headquarters.

Apart from changing the name of the North American company, I decided to fix the fact that our galleries were not open on weekends, which was just another example of the way we'd been ignoring the private client. The concept of only opening from 9:00 a.m. to 5:30 p.m. on weekdays but remaining closed during the two crucial days when many of our best potential clients would have been able to visit the gallery seemed to me to have been embedded in the old way of doing business. "That's what we've always done," was not an answer I tolerated. I knew we needed to usher Sotheby's into a new era and bring it to a place of greater profitability. But even as we began to open our galleries on weekends, I instituted the change in a way that made sense for people. Not every employee needed to work on every weekend; rather, during a weekend when old masters were previewed, for example, only that department would be on duty, and likewise, when it was the turn of Chinese works of art, only the relevant department would come in.

Another way of offending private clients was the way the catalogs were sent out to our customers, frequently arriving only one day before an auction or, even worse, a day *after* the sale had already occurred. This was infuriating to me but I imagine also extremely frustrating to so many of our clients. I decided to centralize catalog production in the New York office and put catalogs to bed one month ahead of each sale. Amid much complaining, I was told by those who opposed the change that we would miss consignments. "For one sale, we might," I would reply, "but after that, people will realize we're serious and get their consignments in by the new deadlines." I was right, and people shifted their usual practices to meet our deadlines. The result was a dramatic increase in private client buying since they now had time to get advice from museum experts and others on works they might want to buy.

We also went to work on the catalogs themselves, which had been incredibly poorly designed and edited. Up to that point, the estimates for items in our catalogs did not appear alongside their corresponding paintings or objects but instead at the back of the book. Items we featured were not described in any detail, leaving customers uninformed. And, among other things, most items did not even appear in color. To me, it was a wonder we managed to sell anything, and I was not pleased with the way the catalogs represented our quality or brand. Following a redesign, we saw dramatic growth in *paid* subscriptions to our catalogs. They actually became a profitable line of business. Our catalogs became beautiful keepsakes and worthy of the good image of Sotheby's I wanted to project as we worked to modernize the company.

As I walked around Sotheby's in my early days, it also seemed to me that we were selling a lot of junk. My McKinsey training led me to raise questions about the lots we were selling. I questioned how many of our annual volume of 300,000 lots worldwide sold for under $1,000. Each lot, I came to understand, was a transaction that needed the same tracking and paperwork, no matter what its size or value. In other words, a lot worth $500, perhaps an unimportant brown wood table or a small piece of jewelry, would require almost as much time and effort as an important painting that could fetch millions. After a little more digging around, I learned that each lot required thirty-five different pieces of paper, from consignment to ultimate sale. I asked for a complete breakdown and, after about six weeks, was told that about one-half of our transactions, or 150,000 lots, were valued at under $1,000. And what percentage of our sales volume did they bring in? A genuinely shocked chief financial officer reported back, after three more weeks of rummaging around, that it was only 4% of our worldwide sales. It was obvious to me that if half of our workload resulted in only 4% of our sales, small lots were killing us as a company and we needed to make some changes. So we immediately raised to $1,000 the minimum value of any object we would accept for sale, with coins and wine being the only exceptions.

It was amazing how much more time everyone had once we made this change. When I first arrived at Sotheby's, all our departments had been screaming for more staff because they said they were overworked. But now, with half their lots eliminated, they found they had enough time to do what they should have been doing in the first place. Instead of selling a lot of junk, they started getting out and meeting people and developing relationships with private clients. It was a remarkable shift, and people were much happier.

These were just a few of the fundamental changes needed at the world's oldest auction house. There were a great many other far-reaching changes that I knew Sotheby's needed during what I believed could be a pivotal moment in the company's history. But none of them would have happened had I not established a good working relationship with the new owner. I had no qualms about working for Al Taubman, whom I knew by reputation to be a difficult personality. I felt my people skills would enable me to deal with him, and for many years, this proved to be the case. A major reason for the ease with which I worked with Alfred lay in the fact that while he might complain about some of the things I wanted to do, he never forbade me to do them. I was never overruled, which is always a great confidence booster for a CEO. And he never once made me do something I did not want to do. This aspect of our relationship would take on even more significance later during the price-fixing case.

I was aware, however, that my way of doing things frustrated Taubman at times because he was a stickler for detail and, loving art as he did, wanted to be involved in all sorts of things he should perhaps have stayed away from, like complaining about the lighting on a piece of jewelry in Geneva or criticizing the catalog photo of a set of dining chairs in Australia. Taubman was into the minutia of the business, and that was not always easy to deal with. While I believed in letting our people make decisions and living with the results, he had no qualms about micromanaging and frequently making life miserable for me and our experts around the company.

At the same time that his eye for financial details left much to be desired, he was a grand visionary who had a clear idea of the unique market opportunity that Sotheby's possessed. As earlier stated, he understood, as I did, that we were selling to the wrong customer. We needed to sell to private clients.

When Taubman bought Sotheby's, it was operating as a wholesaler, selling mostly to art dealers. In fact, most of our clients were dealers who doubled the price of what they bought at auction and sold it on to private collectors. Art dealers loved our practices because we made it virtually impossible for private collectors to be active auction buyers. Taubman even had a name for this; he called it "threshold resistance," and he named his book as such after he later got out of jail for the price-fixing scandal.[3] By threshold resistance, he meant that Sotheby's had made it difficult for a private collector to come in our doors. We made them feel uninformed and stupid, and it was far easier for them to go to an art dealer who would hold their hand and make them comfortable about entering the exotic world of art collecting, even if the art dealer charged them a huge premium compared to the prices they would have paid in auction.

Over the decades, this had created a situation where dealers, much to their satisfaction, ruled the salesroom. They loved being a little mysterious and in control. Private clients were not really welcome, and those who somehow did break through found themselves in dingy, poorly lit salerooms. Dealers loved it this way because, with little interference, they could ensure that private clients could not bid against each other. In this way, they could get together over a coffee before a sale and agree to put a lid on the price. Then they would meet again afterward and have a knockout auction among themselves, leading to a more realistic price level. But of course, the proceeds would not go to the original seller. It was illegal and a restraint of trade and, on both sides of the Atlantic, a felony. Yet, it happened all the time and was a problem industry-wide.

But Taubman, who was a serious art collector himself, saw the opportunity of having Sotheby's sell directly to private clients like himself. He loved the idea of this, but, apart from spending time in London shooting birds on the weekend and redesigning our galleries, he had no idea of how to put this kind of transformation into effect. What he wished to do would be part of a dramatic upward turn in the company's fortunes, but it would require a change in overall strategy that would reorganize the whole ethos of our working life. While Taubman was good at buying assets, he did not know how to manage this level of change. Thankfully, this was my forte, and this is why we worked well as a team.

One change we made had to do with traveling exhibitions. Rather than waiting for people to come to us, we started sending some of our best offerings to Palm Beach, Tokyo, and Hong Kong. This created new buyers around the world. It dramatically improved our ability to serve private clients, and that was quickly reflected in our auction sales. Japanese buyers became a huge factor in the business, and we not only saw new markets open but also new possibilities.

A big difference between auction houses and art dealers had to do with payment terms. Art dealers sold on extended payment terms. We did not. So we created a new company, Sotheby's Financial Services, that enabled us to lend money against works of art, giving buyers an extra six months to a year to come up with 50% of what they owed; either that or they could get a consignor advance of one-half the value of their art and sell in upcoming sales, settling the loan after the auction. Along with Citibank, we became the primary art lender in the world. Utilizing the commercial paper markets, we built up our art loan portfolio to more than $400 million.

So how did we change Sotheby's? We freed up time for our experts to reach out to clients. We began to hand carry works of art around the world. We got catalogs out early. We made our galleries the fun, social place to be on weekends and at opening receptions. We provided financing to ease the immediate cash demands of collecting. Through these and many other changes in antiquated practices, we began to break down the "threshold resistance" and bring private collectors into our salerooms. In fact, they became more than 75% of our buyers. We had become the art retailer we aspired to be.

As one would expect, the art dealer's world changed, and they responded. Art trade shows, such as Art Basel, became commonplace. This was a good thing since more buyers came into the market. But increasingly, private buyers came to the two global auction houses as a way to build their collections. Without question, the innovation of Sotheby's in the '80s led to the global art market that is thriving today.

12

Unconventional Approaches

B RINGING SOTHEBY'S INTO A NEW era and transforming the art world required innovative thinking, risk-taking, and a challenging of the status quo. We were, in many ways, entering unchartered territory, but the potential in the global art market was huge. These major shifts in our business approach brought amazing change, exciting opportunities, and many experiences I'll never forget.

...

IN THE ART WORLD, an "old master" refers to a painting or masterpiece created by one of the most recognized European artists of the thirteenth to seventeenth centuries. When I took over at Sotheby's, I quickly saw that growth markets were hard to find in the art market; new old masters and impressionist works were no longer being created, so the opportunities in this space were limited. But, I realized, jewelry was another case. Though I knew that jewelry was constantly being created by designers at Tiffany, Cartier, Van Cleef, and many others, I observed that "previously owned" jewelry had little cachet in the auction room. This, to me, was a huge market opportunity.

So I set about helping us find ways to bring big buyers to our sales. We hired Bain & Company, the prestigious management consultants (I tried to hire McKinsey, but Taubman knew I had worked there and vetoed the idea) to help us reposition Sotheby's in the jewelry market, and they did an excellent job. Among other strategies, viewing rooms were put in for customers to try on jewelry, and we began to hold elegant luncheons during which ladies could see and wear the jewelry.

But most importantly, we won the mandate to sell the spectacular jewels of the Duchess of Windsor. This, we recognized, was the perfect opportunity for us to change perceptions of the jewelry-buying world, so we did it with abandon. The catalog for the Jewels of the Duchess of Windsor sale was a social history of the duchess's life, full of photos of her wearing each piece, including a narrative about the piece, the place or circumstances under which she acquired it, and when possible a vellum foldout of the piece's original design. The catalog is still a collector's item. The sale was to be held in Geneva, but we marketed the sale globally, exhibiting the pieces in New York, Los Angeles, and elsewhere around the world. As a result, what originally began as a plan for an event of 800 attendees grew quickly with more than 2,000 clients wanting to attend.

In anticipation of the sale, I held weekly planning meetings to connect our jewelry and marketing staff in New York, London, and Geneva. We had all the finest of details taken care of as the date approached, but when, a month before the sale, I asked on our Monday planning meeting if we had a backup generator on hand for the sale, my question was met with laughter. It was Switzerland, I was told, where power never fails. I didn't want to take any chances, so I insisted that we rent one by the following week. A truck-mounted generator was located at the cost of $40,000, and in those days before the event, it came to be dubbed "Ainslie's Folly."

On the date of the sale, April 2, 1987, the excitement was palpable. This was a widely publicized and highly anticipated event. In a large tent across from the beautiful Hotel Beau Rivage on the quai du Mont-Blanc in Geneva, more than 2,000 clients in black tie had gathered for this stand-ing-room-only occasion. The presale estimate of $7–$9 million for this famous jewelry was considered ludicrously low, and there was a general buzz among attendees because they believed that anything could happen in this unprecedented event.

Moments before the sale began, Nicholas Rayner, the auctioneer, announced that the emergency lighting was being tested, so the lights would dim for a moment. They dimmed, came back, and no one thought anything of it, including me. The sale then proceeded, with Rayner switching seamlessly from French to Spanish, Italian to English. Prices were going for six, eight, and ten times the estimates, since everyone wanted a piece of British royal history. In the end, the Windsor jewels brought the remarkable total of $50.1 million. We had made art auction history in doing a sale like this. And the Pasteur Institute, as the beneficiary of the jewelry sale, was extremely pleased.

I had a good laugh when I gave Rayner a congratulatory bear hug afterward, and he whispered in my ear that the entire sale had been conducted on Ainslie's Folly, my generator. It turned out that the scores of TV light bars there to capture the event had been frying the electrical cables running back to the hotel.

Because of our success that day, "previously owned" jewelry had been launched into a new realm of estate jewelry, and prior ownership or provenance became paramount in auction sales. Jewelry, previously only a small part of Sotheby's annual turnover, moved up in importance as a major business line, directly behind impressionist art and contemporary art. It brought and continues to bring great growth to the company.

...

EARLY ON IN MY career at Sotheby's, I knew we were in a unique position to do some good. When Robert Woolley, the head of all decorative arts, came to my office one day in 1985 with an unusual request, I was still new to my role and just settling into the company. "We need to support this new organization called the American Foundation for AIDS Research (amfAR) by doing an auction," said Woolley. He was an openly gay man who had the courage to push for AIDS research during a time when this disease was highly stigmatized. "Many artists and many of us here at Sotheby's are gay, and this new plague of AIDS is a scourge we must help end," he told me.

After much discussion, during which he taught me a great deal about the AIDS epidemic, I agreed we needed to hold a Sotheby's auction as the first-ever fundraiser for amfAR. We planned and promoted the auction, and Woolley set out to get paintings donated by leading contemporary artists.

One week before the auction, Woolley reappeared and said he needed me to come down to the gallery to see one of the paintings being offered. "I am afraid this may appear in *The New York Times*," he told me. He had succeeded in procuring a Keith Haring painting called *Safe Sex* but was concerned because it showed two male stick figures stroking each other. I said, "Robert, there is no turning back now. Whatever happens, happens." He and I laughed, and thankfully nothing later appeared in the press.

The auction was a huge success, raising more than $5 million for amfAR and putting it on the map as the leading AIDS research organization. Though, sadly, Robert Woolley himself died of AIDS some years later, I was grateful we were able to do our part to help end the scourge, and the event and our efforts remain one of my most favorite memories at Sotheby's. They continue to inform me and the opportunities I pursue today.

Whenever possible, I try to align the work I do with things of genuine meaning and value. In future years when I served on the board of Lehman Brothers, for example, I convinced management to hire Posse Foundation scholars as interns. For several summers, fifty young Posse students had the opportunity to work at Lehman. Many of them joined the company permanently upon graduation.

...

DURING MY YEARS AT Sotheby's, few of our transactions were more contentious than the trading in ivory. Despite laws that were supposed to safeguard elephant herds in Africa and Asia, elephants were still being picked off by poachers all over these continents, and environmental groups in the late '80s had been making themselves heard in defense of this beautiful animal. At the time, one of the poachers' tricks was to chemically treat ivory so that it appeared to be forty to fifty years old rather than more recently poached.

I knew that ivory was a favorite commodity among serious collectors, but it became clear to me that in facilitating the sale of ivory, Sotheby's was inadvertently acting as a fence for poachers, and both the company and poachers were making a handsome profit from it. Ethically, I could not defend such a practice. There was a lot of discussion within the firm over this, and I eventually made the decision that Sotheby's would no longer sell any ivory unless it could be proven to be at least a hundred years old.

Even though this new policy I set did not lead to a great loss of business, Al Taubman was initially furious and accused me of caving in to environmental critics. But when I remained firm with the decision, he backed down and went along with it.

It so happened that right around the time I made this policy switch, Sotheby's was in the process of selling two pairs of tusks for Saul Steinberg, a major collector of old masters. Steinberg had begun making his fortune in his twenties by leasing out IBM computers, undercutting IBM in the process.[1] He went on to become CEO of Reliance Insurance and tried to buy Walt Disney Productions at one stage of his career. Steinberg was not the sort of man you wanted to mess about with, but it was clear to me that we hadn't done our homework and had signed a consignment agreement with him to sell the tusks. Since the tusks were clearly less than a hundred years old, I couldn't back down on a much-trumpeted new policy, so I had to make an awkward phone call.

"We're not going to be able to sell the tusks," I said when Steinberg came on the line.

"The hell you're not!" came his predictable reply.

It was a difficult conversation, but when I offered to have Sotheby's buy the tusks at the middle estimate of around $50,000 for each pair and donate them to a natural history museum, Steinberg agreed to let go of the sale and was, I think, quite pleased with the ultimate outcome. I've always believed in the value of sticking to one's position but having a good backup plan prepared. I was glad to have been able to craft a compromise that allowed Sotheby's to maintain a positive relationship with a good client.

Years later in 2012, partly because of the decision we made to honor our relationship with our client, Sotheby's ended up selling many millions' worth of art when Saul Steinberg's entire collection came up for sale upon his death.

...

IN 1988, JUST AS Communism was coming to an end, I decided that Sotheby's should undertake the first-ever auction in Moscow. Our director, Baron Hans Heinrich Thyssen-Bornemisza, industrialist and art collector, had been working on an exchange with the Hermitage Museum in St. Petersburg (or Leningrad, as it was known then). The baron, whose own wonderful collection now resides at the Thyssen-Bornemisza National Museum in Madrid, was offering to lend some of his paintings, which were then housed near his home in Lugano, Switzerland, to the Hermitage. He had been discussing the project with Raisa Gorbachev, wife of Mikhail Gorbachev, and the subject of Russian artists came up. Although the harsher aspects of Communism were slowly being eased under her husband's relatively enlightened leadership, artists living in the Soviet Union were still finding it impossible to sell their work and gain any recognition unless they followed the Communist Party line. These "unofficial artists," as they were called, were talented but little known and impoverished Russian painters. They had been going against the government rules that only allowed the painting of Soviet Realism, and instead they painted abstract, contemporary, satirical, even political art.

It did not sit well with Raisa Gorbachev that hundreds of artists were having to work illegally and were virtually penniless. When she asked how to get these artists known, Baron Thyssen suggested that Sotheby's could perhaps stage an auction in Moscow so that their work could be brought up from the cellars and catacombs where many of them painted and be exhibited on the world stage.

I thought this was a great idea, but Al Taubman blew a fuse. With his East German / Polish background, he was particularly sensitive to the subject of dealing with Communist states. I explained to him that we would simply be helping starving artists and was happy to receive enthusiastic backing for this idea from our London chairman, Lord Gowrie, who sent several London experts to Moscow to evaluate the work of these "illegal" artists. Taubman, who was known to strongly object to some of my initiatives, eventually came around after a serious amount of grumbling.

Forty artists put up their work—avant-garde and other pieces of Soviet art—for this historic and groundbreaking auction. The sale was to be conducted in Moscow in pounds sterling, with bidders in the saleroom and with others calling in from around the world, and all the proceeds were to go to the artists. Everything appeared to be going smoothly until a government official informed us that the government intended to pay the artists not in sterling but in rubles at the official exchange rate to the pound. We knew this would be hugely beneficial to the Soviet government since it would receive hard currency in British pounds but only have to pay out near-worthless rubles to the struggling artists. The Soviets, desperate for hard currency, seemed unmoved on the subject until we told them flatly that we would pack up and cancel the auction unless they compromised. After some stiff negotiations, we agreed that the artists would be paid out at the golden ruble rate, a rate used often, we learned, for business transactions and which was five times the official ruble rate. With the black-market rate being ten times the official rate, we ensured the artists made some money.

The auction was a huge success and a lifesaver for many of the artists, some of whom are now represented in London and Paris. Composer Andrew Lloyd Webber bought *Fundamental Lexicon*, a painting by artist Grisha Brushkin, for £500,000, and many other pieces went for well over their estimate. I'm proud of the work we did to advocate for these artists and open up new avenues of growth for Sotheby's in Russia. Today, there's a Sotheby's Moscow office that has held more than twenty international exhibitions.

Preparation of the rostrum for the groundbreaking Sotheby's auction in Moscow, July 7, 1988. Michael Ainslie is standing with Lord Gowrie, chairman of Sotheby's Europe in the back left.

...

THERE WERE MANY OTHER memorable moments I had at Sotheby's, but I will always look back on the lunch I was able to share with Queen Elizabeth, the Queen Mother, at the Bond Street headquarters of our

London office as a particularly enjoyable occasion. One of our board members was Grey Ruthven, the 2nd Earl of Gowrie. I had approached Grey for him to become chairman of Sotheby's in London because I felt we needed to have stronger connections with the moneyed aristocracy in the United Kingdom, and he was certainly not short of connections. He considered the Queen Mother to be one of his greatest friends and advisors, so it was a great honor for all of us when she accepted Grey's lunch invitation.

Boardroom lunches were an old tradition at Sotheby's in both London and New York, and major clients and important dignitaries were always treated to elegant fare by our chefs. It was obviously going to be a special occasion, so Al Taubman and his wife, Judy, arranged to be in London for the Queen Mother's visit. She arrived in a hat bejeweled with incredible emeralds, escorted by Lord King, then chairman of British Airways. She had elected to come on a day when Chinese works of art were to be auctioned in the early afternoon, so Julian Thompson, our senior Chinese expert and chairman of Sotheby's Asia, joined us for the lunch until he had to depart to begin the auction.

Following a pleasant luncheon, we were all enjoying dessert and coffee when the company's large leather guest book was passed around for everyone to sign. After Taubman signed the book, he passed it on to the Queen Mother but, in doing so, allowed the heavy leather cover of the book to fall from his grasp and land on the edge of her demitasse saucer, flipping a few drops of the remaining coffee in her cup onto the beautiful vellum page of the book. Without missing a beat, the Queen Mother picked up the blotting paper—of course the Brits would have a blotter in the guest book—and blotted the coffee spots, remarking, "You know, when they had floods in Venice, we sent blotting paper from England to dry their important books." Putting people at ease in awkward moments was one of the Queen Mother's most appreciated talents, and I was relieved to be able to witness it at close quarters. And I am certain Taubman was as well.

Suzanne and Michael Ainslie meeting HRH Queen Elizabeth
at a reception, Fall 1988. Photo credit: Barry Swaede.

After lunch, I took her on a tour of the back of the house at Sotheby's. In the rabbit warren of back halls, we came upon a young expert intensely cataloging a painting. She was the most shocked person in the United Kingdom when she looked up to find the Queen Mother, probably the next most recognizable person in the country after Queen Elizabeth II, peering at the computer screen over her shoulder. "Now, my dear, don't let me interrupt you," said the Queen Mother. "I just wanted to see how you do this."

And on we trotted, arriving upstairs just as Julian Thompson was hammering down a Chinese pot from his auction podium above a packed saleroom. "Oh, there he is," stated the Queen Mother in a stage whisper just loud enough to bring all eyes in the room to see her looking through a door near the front of the gallery. After watching a few lots be sold—at higher prices than they would have fetched if she had not been standing there—we moved toward our Bond Street entrance where her car and driver awaited.

Emerging onto Bond Street, which the police had closed to traffic, we were met by thunderous applause from hundreds of onlookers and scores of construction workers, the latter hanging on to the scaffolding of a building that was being renovated across Bond Street. There were no cheers or cheeky comments; I just heard loud and respectful applause, reflecting the deep affection people had for her. She threw kisses to them all, bade me farewell, and disappeared into her classic Daimler, leaving us all with a feeling of warmth and delight from her day at Sotheby's.

. . .

Michael Ainslie speaking with President Reagan at a New York Stock Exchange luncheon, explaining his recent Dupuytren's surgery, fall 1989. Standing alongside are Richard Grasso (president of the New York Stock Exchange) and Bill Donaldson (chairman of the Securities and Exchange Commission), and in the background is Robert Rubin, the former CEO of Goldman Sachs and secretary of the treasury.

SOTHEBY'S OPENED THE DOOR to many incredible opportunities for me personally. I was able to meet and work with fascinating people. I truly enjoyed and received much satisfaction from using my skills and background to guide and transform the art auction world. It proved to me that the keys to productive change are humility, asking lots of questions, and engaging the existing team in finding the answers.

I once took my father to meet Al Taubman at his elegant New York apartment. Dad immediately asked him, "Mr. Taubman, why did you hire Mike?"

Taubman quickly responded, "I hired Michael because he is smart, and he has good manners." His answer made my father feel good and may help explain why we had such great success in changing a very old, stuffy institution.

13

The Building of the Top Auction House

LOVED THE CHALLENGE OF REESTABLISHING Sotheby's as the top auction house, and the financial results we saw were staggering. In the five years after I arrived in 1984, our yearly sales exploded from $600 million to $2.9 billion. And our annual profits grew even more dramatically, going from $3 million to $113 million. Clearly, by 1989, we dominated the auction market.

We quickly paid off the $65 million that Al Taubman had borrowed from Chase Manhattan to finance half of his $130 million acquisition price, and we began to pay substantial dividends to Taubman and the ten or twelve partners he had brought in as investors in 1983. But several of the investors became impatient to cash out, so in the spring of 1987, our board decided it was time to take Sotheby's public again.

To go public, we had some work to do. For several years, I had been the only executive with stock options. When Taubman was recruiting me for my job, I'd rejected his initial offer of a 2% stock option on the basis that I would be taking a considerable risk with an ailing company. The offer was negotiated up to options on 4% of the stock, and at the last minute, Jeffrey Miro, Taubman's lawyer, had offered a matching stock appreciation right, known as a SAR, which provided for a cash payment matching the gain on the options to be paid at the time of stock option exercises. The SAR enabled the holder to have the cash to pay the taxes on the gain on the options. In theory, the SAR holder would not have to sell stock to pay the taxes and could retain all the stock.

Taubman and his lawyers decided that my SAR needed to be repurchased by the company before we went public, so we entered into a negotiation in the summer of 1987. They asked what I wanted to sell it back to the company. It was difficult to put a value on this SAR because I knew that it only had full value when my stock vested, which was not for another five years, since Taubman had insisted on an unusual ten-year vesting period for my stock options.

It was clear that the SAR had substantial value, as the stock had greatly appreciated. So, after much calculating, I said I would sell the SAR back to the company for $10 million and was delighted when Jeffrey Miro quickly said yes. In fact, he said yes so quickly that I feared I had underpriced it. Nonetheless, we began drawing up the documents for the public offering with full disclosure of the SAR repurchase by the company.

Since Sotheby's was a private company, my compensation agreement had not been made public. Taubman came to me after we'd reached agreement and said, "Michael, you realize the announcement of this SAR sale will cause a firestorm in the company, since you are the only one getting this kind of a payout."

I told him, "Yes, Alfred, I've given this much thought, and it is clear to me that the senior management team has had much to do with our turnaround and will feel this isn't equitable. But, I have an idea. I'll contribute $3 million of my $10 million to a 'going public' bonus for the top thirty or so senior executives and experts if you will match it, giving us a $6 million pool, and we will pay out substantial bonuses to them at the same time."

"That sounds like a good plan. The company will match your $3 million," Taubman responded. "Include that in the prospectus for the public offering. I'm off to spend some time in Greece with my good friend George Livanos, and you and I can review it all when I get back."

Unfortunately, selective memory was a trait Taubman was known for, and upon his return from Greece, he looked at the documents and shocked me by stating, "I never agreed to match you. If you want to do that, go ahead, but the company is not putting up any money to increase the pool."

Astonished by this betrayal, I proceeded ahead with my side of the $3 million bonus pool. Each person on the senior management team received a bonus that ranged from $100,000 to $350,000 for his or her part in helping in the company turnaround. As I shared the good news about the special going-public bonuses with each person, I did not hold back in stating that I wished the amount could have been more, but the company had decided not to participate in the pool and it was coming from a restructuring of my SAR, an agreement I had negotiated more than four years earlier upon joining Sotheby's. Most members of the management team were extremely appreciative and made that evident. While I was disappointed by Taubman's non-participation, I also saw that the result of the bonus program was unifying to management and enabled us to work as an even closer team going forward.

After a global road show, working with Alex Brown and Lazard as our underwriters, Sotheby's went public on May 13, 1988. Stock that Taubman and his investor group had bought for $1.35 a share in 1983 was now trading for $12.50 per share, and several original investors were able to have the liquidity they sought.

It had taken the better part of three years for me to persuade Taubman to also offer options to about half of the 1,500 Sotheby's employees in London, New York, and elsewhere who, previously, had been poorly paid, to say the least. Given their salaries and no stock, most could not afford to get married and raise a family, which was something that I knew had to change. When I finally convinced Taubman, largely with help from Max Fisher, one of the company's investors and the vice chairman of the board, that we needed a broad-based stock option program for Sotheby's employees, several hundred senior and mid-level staff received substantial stock option grants under a new stock option plan put in place in 1987. After we went public, many Sotheby's staff members had share options that were worth $1 million or more, and hundreds of other employees had a sizeable stake in the company.

It became clear to me later on that Taubman had always felt I got the better of him in the negotiation of my original contract four years earlier because never, over the next ten years, was I granted a further share option, which was unusual. Also, my colleagues told me of frequent complaining from Taubman and his lawyers about the "bad deal they had made with Michael." I have a strong belief that it is a really good thing if incentives are aligned and everyone makes money when a business does well. Sadly, the simple idea of a win-win was not in Taubman's mind-set. He seemed to feel that if I was doing well financially from the company's success, it was coming out of his pocket.

In many ways, the SAR sale and the Sotheby's IPO (initial public offering) marked the beginning of the end of my healthy working relationship with Taubman. For five years, as a private company, we had little press coverage about the business side of Sotheby's. But this changed dramatically with the announced plan for an IPO. Suddenly, everyone wanted to write about the remarkable turnaround in the company's fortunes. Taubman, as chairman and 60% stockholder, was featured in these stories, but as the CEO who had led the turnaround, so was I. And it did not sit well with him. When one major article in *Business Week* referred to him as a "cigar chomping real estate developer from Detroit" and to me as a "tall, urbane Tennessean," the temperature in our relationship cooled substantially.

. . .

SOTHEBY'S PUBLIC OFFERING IN 1988 was followed by an amazing year in 1989 with auction sales growth of 60%, from $1.8 billion to $2.9 billion. But it was too good to last forever. What goes up so fast often comes down just as rapidly. The summer of 1990 marked the end of the biggest art market boom ever seen. The Japanese economy stalled, their banks stopped lending, and Japanese buyers stopped coming to auctions. They had been our biggest buyers, particularly of impressionist paintings. American and European real estate developers got caught in a credit crunch and disappeared from the saleroom. Our worldwide auction sales plummeted from almost $3 billion to a low of $1.1 billion in 1991.

Early in 1990, Sotheby's put out a guarantee of $50 million to win the consignment of the collection of Henry Ford, our former director, who had passed away in 1989. By the time we held the auction in November 1990, the art market had weakened dramatically, and several of Ford's paintings did not sell. The stock market was so nervous about our potential losses from this guarantee that trading in our stock was not allowed the following day until I went public with a midmorning announcement that quantified our exposure as only a possible $5 million loss.

Given the dramatic downturn in auction sales, the company went into a major cost reduction program. Over the next eighteen months, we cut operating costs by $40 million, or about 17% of our total costs.

Most difficult was getting our colleagues in London to take cost cutting seriously. Their attitude seemed to be, "We made lots of money in the past several years, so why should we have to cut costs now?" It became evident that I needed to be present in London to make this happen. I decided to move to London with my wife, Suzanne, for a year in 1991. During this time, we made plans to close one of our regional salerooms in Chester and reduce the number of staff in Europe and London. Through these necessary measures and others, Sotheby's was able to remain profitable despite a 70% reduction in auction sales and a failing global art market.

I knew that cutting staff further would seriously impede the company's ability to serve clients as the market slowly recovered, and we needed to find a way to create new revenue. According to our model of business, auction income for Sotheby's was made up of two parts, a seller's commission and a buyer's premium commission. The commission charged to the seller was negotiable and had been steadily declining as competition for consignments with our rival, Christie's, heated up. During the years leading up to the market downturn, the average seller's commission had declined from an average of 8% down to about 6%, but the buyer's premium, or BP, was nonnegotiable and stood at 10%.

I began to shape a radical idea. I realized that sellers have options about where they're going to sell and frequently go with the auction house that offers the lowest selling commission. But buyers don't have the same option. If Sotheby's is selling the Picasso they want for their collection, they have to buy it from Sotheby's, and paying a few extra dollars in BP is not going to deter them from bidding. I saw that we had pricing power with buyers and not with sellers, so to get new revenue, we could increase the nonnegotiable part of our auction income, the BP, which up to that point had been well established at 10% for the past thirteen years.

My studies at Vanderbilt had concentrated on math and economics, so I took on the design of the BP changes as a math problem. As I tackled the math and thought through the different scenarios, I had two goals: one, to make the change so desirable that Christie's would be compelled to follow us after we announced the change, and two, to design a BP that was flexible and could be easily altered in the years to come. It was apparent that the seller's commission would continue to be under competitive pressure, so I wanted to be smart in the way I designed the BP. I also knew that whatever we implemented had to be done with no consultation with our competitor, since that was illegal.

Working principally with my CFO Russell Roth, we came up with a BP that would generate substantial new revenue for Sotheby's. The BP would increase to 15% on lots sold for under $50,000. On lots of higher value, 15% would be charged on the first $50,000, and the existing BP of 10% would be charged on the value above $50,000. As a result, the maximum BP increase on any one purchase would be 5% of $50,000, or $2,500. We were hopeful this would not deter a buyer who saw a property at Sotheby's he or she wanted. Because we knew that the cumulative annual amount of new BP revenue, projected at $25 million, would have a major impact on our bottom line, we were hopeful Christie's would follow with a similar BP pricing structure.

Sotheby's announced the BP increase in November 1992, to become effective on January 1, 1993. Then we waited to see what Christie's would do. Seven weeks went by with no word. Then suddenly, Christie's announced it would make a similar BP change, effective March 1, 1993. Apparently our rival realized that we would have lots of new income to be even more competitive in negotiating the seller's commission. Note that it is not illegal to have identical pricing, but it *is* illegal to agree to the pricing in advance. This important nuance would become significant later in the price-fixing scandal brought on by the collusion between then Sotheby's CEO Diana D. Brooks, known to everyone as Dede, her childhood name, and Christie's CEO Christopher Davidge.

Fast-forward to today, and exactly as I anticipated, Sotheby's BP structure has been altered several times over the past two decades and three times in the past three years. At the time of this writing, the latest increase became effective on February 25, 2019. The charge is now 25% on the first $400,000 of the hammer price, 20% on the portion of the hammer price greater than $400,000 and through $4 million, and 13.9% above $4 million.[1] To give an example, on a $5 million painting, the BP at Sotheby's today would be $959,000 or 19.18%. Under our original 1992 BP, the commission on a $5 million painting would have been $502,500, or 10.05%. The new flexible pricing model worked, and the buyer at auction is paying most of the freight today. Christie's has a similar, though not identical, BP pricing structure.

It is worth pointing out that as I predicted, the seller's commission has further eroded and is frequently 2% or even zero today as reliance on the BP has increased. However, even at 19% plus a small seller's commission, the cost of buying at auction is much lower than it would be from an art dealer who generally charges a markup of 40% to 50% of the value of the object.

My Vanderbilt math and economics education paid off. It allowed Sotheby's to not only survive the temporary collapse of the global art market but to also continue to remain profitable through the art market recession of the early '90s. I'm pleased that we were able to clearly establish a new pricing paradigm for the auction industry that has continued to evolve with competitive pressures. These and other efforts are part of the reason that Sotheby's remains one of the two top auction houses today. Ironically, Sotheby's announced on June 17, 2019 that a wealthy art collector, Patrick Drahi, would lead a group to buy the company and take it private.[2] This replicates what Taubman and his investor group did in 1983 some 36 years earlier, but this time with an enterprise value of $3.7 billion, as opposed to Taubman's purchase price of $130 million. The compound annual return for these 36 years is 9.75%, so we must have done some things right in bringing Sotheby's into the modern era. The challenge of modernizing this long-standing institution has been one of the most rewarding experiences of my life.

14

Behind the Scenes

WORKED WITH MANY TALENTED, HARDWORKING individuals in my years at Sotheby's, including an amazing group of board members and many world-class experts who were key to our operations. Managing really talented people is what I love. I greatly value the lessons I learned through my interactions with Al Taubman, Sotheby's board members, and so many others at Sotheby's who shaped my experience in ways I'll never forget.

In my earliest years, the changes in strategy we brought to Sotheby's made a big and positive impact on the company and, though Taubman sometimes carped about my decisions, both he and the board seemed pleased with my leadership. In many ways, Taubman treated me like a son and, since I was a newly divorced bachelor at the time I started with the company, he helped me socialize around New York. I always worked hard to establish good relationships with him and the board members, and many of the board members also made me feel like a part of the family over the years.

Early board members included Max Fisher, an American businessman and philanthropist; Ann Getty, the interior designer and philanthropist; Bill Pitt of William Pitt Realty; Gianni Agnelli, the Italian industrialist and head of Fiat; Baron Hans Heinrich Thyssen-Bornemisza, the industrialist and art collector; Grey Ruthven, the 2nd Earl of Gowrie; Henry

Ford, the grandson of the founder of the Ford Motor Company; and Earl Smith, a larger-than-life character who had been the US ambassador to Cuba just before Castro came to power in 1959 and then who later served as mayor of Palm Beach. Taubman also relied heavily on the advice of Leslie Wexner, who at a young age created the clothing companies The Limited and Victoria's Secret.[1]

It was an honor and a constant challenge for me to work among such powerful business leaders and people of influence.

...

BEFORE THE COMPANY WENT public in 1989, Max Fisher, a close and longtime friend of Taubman's and one of the original investors in the company, served as the vice chairman of the board. He was once described by another board member as having "a bear trap for a brain who could smell BS a mile away." Though he knew little about art himself, he was essential to Sotheby's financial health. Much more so than Taubman, he was a stern taskmaster on financial discipline and was demanding when it came to setting and meeting budgets. Max insisted that the executive committee, made up of Taubman, him, and me, approve any loan commitment greater than $5 million. And because of his friendship with Taubman, he was able to talk freely with him. I felt that Max, with his intellect and likeable manner, always offered good counsel to Taubman and others.

I appreciated having Max looking after our interests and felt he certainly looked after mine. I became fond of him during the time we worked together and found him to be thoughtful, caring, and wise. He would always respond on the occasions when I would go to him for help and advice. "Is Taubman into Ainslie-bashing mode again?" was his customary reply in the later years after things became increasingly more difficult. "I guess Dede has been up to her old tricks, trying to drive a wedge between you two," he'd say, acknowledging the divisive actions of Dede Brooks, who was then the president of Sotheby's North America, one of our five operating companies. Max played a major part in my career at Sotheby's, and I communicated with his wife, Marjorie, after he passed away in 2005,[2] stating how much I respected him and appreciated his constant support over the years.

...

AS I MENTIONED EARLIER, Grey Ruthven, the 2nd Earl of Gowrie, was another board member. I had approached Grey to become chairman of Sotheby's in London. When he, after much negotiation, finally agreed to take the position, he told me that it was essential he first let three people know. I asked him to list them.

"Well, first of all the prime minister," he said. Since he was in Margaret Thatcher's cabinet as minister of culture at the time, I thought this eminently reasonable. "And the second is the Queen Mum. She is one of my greatest friends and advisors, and I always take her into my confidence." I could see no objection to that. "And the third is the monarch," Grey said grandly, looking as if he were about to bow to the queen.

Agreeing to all of that was the easy part, but the prior negotiations up to that point had been somewhat more demanding. In order to avoid the tabloids, we'd met secretly in the splendid London flat of George Weidenfeld, the society publisher, and if Lord Gowrie was not expecting something quite as lavish, he did make it plain that he needed somewhere to live.

"I have been working for years in public service on a government salary of £33,000 a year," he said. "I need a London flat. To buy one, I need one million pounds tax-free." I could see that he was obviously going to be expensive, but with his connections, we felt reasonably confident that this charming fellow, who was also the hereditary chief of the Scottish clan of Ruthven, would bring in sufficient business to compensate. So we flew him on the Concorde to JFK, helicoptered him out to Southampton in Long Island for a cordial lunch with Taubman and me, and did the deal. It was made possible by the fact that British citizens are not required to pay tax on their worldwide income, and in light of that, we kept him traveling for the better part of a year, learning the auction business in New York and elsewhere, and paid him a one-million-pound signing bonus.

I think Grey tried to do his best for us, but two problems arose, one of them quite publicly. *The Sun*, a British tabloid, discovered that he was regularly visiting a massage parlor of dubious repute before he caught his train to his country home in Wales on Friday evenings, and pictures of him exiting the establishment in question were plastered all over the front page.[3] While ordinary British citizens might get away with this kind of behavior, you are tabloid fodder if you're a member of the House of Lords. What was particularly infuriating to the Sotheby's staff was that *The Sun* reported that his visits occurred on Friday afternoons at three or four p.m. when he was clearly on company time. Most American CEOs would have fired him, but I chose to do the opposite. Taking a more subtle approach, I ignored the tabloid coverage and let matters rest for about a year.

But the second problem could not be ignored. For all his charm and contacts in high places, Grey had not been bringing in the kind of business we anticipated. So eventually, once everything had calmed down, I demoted him from executive chairman of Europe to ordinary board member, reducing his pay and time commitment. I think he was appreciative of the manner in which I handled the situation.

Doing the unexpected was a lesson I had learned in my twenties from Jomo Kenyatta when he sent Double O, his political foe, out to western Kenya, rather than to jail or worse. It worked to avoid bloodshed in Kenya, and my similar approach worked to avoid even more embarrassment for Sotheby's and Lord Gowrie. At certain times in life, it's wisest to do what is unexpected in order to allow others to preserve some dignity and avoid further bad publicity.

...

BOARD MEMBER BILL PITT, who became a good friend of mine, was a highly successful real estate developer. He also owned William Pitt Realty, a brokerage firm with offices in all the small and prosperous towns of Fairfield County, Connecticut, like Greenwich, New Canaan, and Westport. After getting to know his operation, I appointed William Pitt Realty as Sotheby's International Realty's official affiliate throughout Fairfield County, but embarrassingly, given our friendly relationship, Pitt Realty did not perform well and was not selling much real estate for us. At some point, our arrangement stopped making sense financially, and I told his firm that it would have to pay a higher annual fee of $50,000.

I was dealing with Peter Healey, his CEO, but quickly got word that Bill was not happy about the increased fee. Weeks went by, and it became clear he was not going to pay it. I took the problem for the third time to Taubman, who had a long-standing friendship with Bill in Palm Beach, since they both had homes there. Inevitably, Taubman was not happy at the thought of severing our business connections with Bill, but I told him it would be necessary if William Pitt Realty did not come up with the increased annual fee of $50,000, and I urged him to talk to Bill.

In the meantime, Stuart Siegel, my CEO of our realty arm, kept warning Healey of the consequences of nonpayment. Still nothing happened. Eventually, we were obliged to tell William Pitt Reality that the relationship was over.

Bill was furious and immediately called Taubman, saying, "How dare you do this! I'm a friend of yours!" To my astonishment, I learned that Taubman, being too afraid to face his friend and give him bad news, had never uttered a word about the problem to Bill. Bill did not take it well, and the incident caused a complete schism among the Palm Beach set, which never healed. Bill and his wife, Pauline, a leading socialite in town, rarely spoke to the Taubmans again, nor did their friends. Taubman had his own coterie of friends, and the two groups simply ignored each other.

I wish the relationship with Bill Pitt had not ended as unfortunately as it did. However, it shows that even powerful and wealthy people like Taubman are sometimes unable to deliver bad news, even to their closest friends.

...

BARON HANS HEINRICH THYSSEN-BORNEMISZA was not only a Sotheby's board member but also the owner of one of the world's greatest art collections. My most memorable meeting with him occurred in 1985 when I was looking for a chairman for Sotheby's Europe. I had my eye on Simon de Pury, who had gained an excellent reputation as curator of the Thyssen Collection, which was then housed at the Villa Favorita in Lugano, Switzerland. When I approached Simon about the position, he expressed interest, but we both knew that nothing could be done without the baron's consent.

So I traveled out to Daylesford, the beautiful Cotswold home in Gloucestershire that Thyssen had bought from newspaper magnate Lord Rothermere some years earlier, to ask Thyssen, as delicately as I could manage, if he would mind us stealing his curator. But on that particular day, he was not immediately available. By chance, August 17, 1985, was the day after his marriage to his fifth wife, Carmen "Tita" Cervera, who was to play a formidable role in the final destination of the art collection, which is now housed in the Thyssen-Bornemisza Museum in Madrid.

The merriment had obviously been considerable, since the baron had not yet risen when I arrived. So I spent much of the afternoon getting acquainted with Tita and members of her family, including her mother and sister. After what seemed like an interminable wait, Thyssen eventually emerged, clad in a velvet smoking jacket, at around eight p.m.

There was nothing to do but to come straight to the point, so I said, "I have come to seek your approval to hire Simon de Pury to become chairman of Sotheby's Europe."

The baron did not seem to be particularly put out by this request and merely replied, "Does Simon want to do this?"

I said that he had indicated that he did, providing the baron had no objections.

"Well, I think he has done most of what he can do for me, so, obviously, this seems like a good opportunity for him. Let me talk to Simon, and I will call you in a few days." And true to his word, he did call and gave me his consent.

Although he preferred not to use the title, Simon was also a baron, born into a Basel family steeped in art. His mother was an expert in ikebana, the Japanese art of flower arrangement, and young Simon studied at the Tokyo Academy of Art before continuing his education at the Sotheby's Institute. His first job had been with Sotheby's, working in London and Monte Carlo, and he opened the company branch in Geneva. So the Sotheby's link made him a natural choice to become chairman of Sotheby's Europe.

It was a successful choice, and Simon quickly gained a reputation as one of the most flamboyant and successful auctioneers in the business, and later, through his frequent appearances on BBC television, he became known as the "Man with the Golden Gavel." Before he left Sotheby's for his next venture, Simon enjoyed what he later described as his "most wonderful moment" when he brought down the gavel on Édouard Manet's *The Absinthe Drinker* in New York in 1995. The pre-estimate had been $12 million, but Simon sold it to the Andrew Lloyd Webber Foundation for $29.1 million.

. . .

ANOTHER INFLUENTIAL MEMBER OF the board was Henry Ford, grandson of the founder of the Ford Motor Company. I grew fond of Henry, who was a good-hearted soul. He was not a man who liked to be surprised, and as chairman of the compensation committee, he wanted to be briefed in detail before each board or compensation committee meeting. This necessitated that I fly out to Detroit eight or nine times a year so that we could script every part of the meeting.

It's interesting to think of how quickly the world's attitude can change; to me, the Sotheby's board provided a perfect example. The grandfathers of Henry Ford and Heini Thyssen were both known anti-Semites who openly supported and assisted Hitler. Yet little more than four decades later, their grandsons sat at the same table on a board chaired, and liberally populated, by Jews, and everyone became genuinely good friends. Sometimes there is hope for humankind.

. . .

OVER THE YEARS, AL Taubman's wife, Judy, included herself in the company's affairs in a way that often created problems. She had worked at Christie's, our greatest competitor, early in her career and was clearly a knowledgeable art person. Before taking the job, I had been warned by someone who knew Taubman well that he had two big weaknesses. One was his inability to stand up to strong women, which I certainly witnessed with Dede Brooks and Judy. Two was his tendency to kowtow to the British aristocracy, a trait that led him to twelve unfortunate and unexplained meetings with Sir Anthony Tennant, the chairman of Christie's. I had already seen firsthand how he enjoyed the company of lords and ladies, a characteristic fostered by Judy's holding of many dinner parties with the "right" people in London and New York. The more she became involved with happenings at Sotheby's, the more difficult my life became.

When Taubman eventually agreed to come to Moscow for the company's first-ever auction, for example, it was clear that Judy was building a distance between Taubman and me. The rift that she was creating became all too evident at the dinner we held the night before the auction. Initially, Taubman told me that he and Judy would not be attending, which was hardly diplomatic, given that we were about to do something truly groundbreaking in Russia. The dinner was not a particularly formal affair, but I had invited the US ambassador and was sitting next to him at our table when suddenly Taubman and Judy walked in. I immediately jumped up and offered my seat, but Taubman waved me away and said they would go over to another table to join some of the artists. Judy, it turned out, was furious about this and later let me know it, ignoring the fact that she and Taubman had rejected my original invitation.

An even bigger problem occurred at an ill-fated dinner that Sotheby's held on another occasion, this time at Apsley House, the home of the Duke of Wellington, which overlooks Hyde Park Corner. The home carries the grand, if unofficial, address of No. 1 London, and the nineteenth-century interior design is as impressive as the works of art that drape its walls.

As far as the 150 guests were concerned, the most publicly embarrassing aspect of the evening was the welcoming speech delivered by the curator of Apsley House who clearly had been overserved during the cocktail hour. Making much ado about the way in which the original Iron Duke, as Wellington was nicknamed after Waterloo, had gone to Spain on horseback and plundered a wonderful collection of paintings from the king of Spain, he went on to announce in thunderous tones, "And let no one ever think that they will be returned to Spain!" Since one of our board members, the king of Spain's sister, Infanta Pilar, the Duchess of Badajoz, was sitting a few feet away, it was a gratuitously insulting remark. Needless to say, she was furious.

Privately, I had to deal with an almost equally unnecessary and insulting situation that evening. Because the guest list was overloaded with notable people from all over the art world, we had decided not to have a head table. Round tables of ten were arranged around the room, and although the intention was to make it look as democratic as possible, there were, inevitably, a couple of tables that were not favorably placed. One was right by the door to the kitchen through which the stream of waiters carried out the food. Judy, to my horror, insisted that Baron Thyssen and his wife, Tita, be seated there. Obviously, I tried to object. Besides being the owner of one of the world's greatest art collections, the baron had become a friend of mine. But Judy was adamant.

Early the following morning, I received a telegram from the baron. It read, "Dear Michael, I hereby resign from the board of Sotheby's. Regards, Heini." I didn't need to be told why. Immediately, I got on the phone and called his flat. I told him that I fully understood his feelings and was extremely sorry. I also made no attempt to dissuade him from his desired course of action but instead asked him one favor.

"Please, Heini," I said, hoping my ruse would work. "I have a very challenging board meeting today that I realize you will not be attending. But could you do me a great favor and not have us announce your resignation until a later date? It would simplify matters for me."

"Oh, okay, I suppose so," he grudgingly replied. The subject was never raised again, and the baron remained on the board for the next fifteen years until he passed away in 2002.

Michael Ainslie talking with Baron Hans Heinrich Thyssen-Bornemisza and Henry Ford II at a Sotheby's board meeting in London, fall 1987. Photo credit: Mattox Commercial Photography.

...

ANOTHER EXPLOSIVE INTERACTION OCCURRED in the spring of 1984 at a Sotheby's board meeting in London. I made it a habit to inform the board of any upcoming sale of a potentially controversial item. In July 1984, we were going to auction the diary of Che Guevara, the Marxist guerilla who assisted Castro in his overthrow of Batista in Cuba. I knew that one of our board members, Ambassador Earl Smith, the last American ambassador to Cuba, would be upset, and he was.

Upon hearing of the impending sale, he pounded the table and shouted, "This is positively un-American."

Having anticipated his anger, I responded with a question. "Earl, do you object because this is 'negative history'?" I asked him.

After blustering a bit, he stammered, "I suppose that is it."

Prepared, I asked him, "Well, we have an Old Masters Department that sells what some would call negative history in its paintings of the crucifixion. Should we close that down as well?"

After a pause, Earl concurred that perhaps it was important history that we should proceed to sell. As it turned out, we were unable to auction the diaries, since the Bolivian government intervened and blocked the sale. Only in 2008 did the Bolivian government finally release the diaries to the public. So, in the final analysis, Earl Smith had his way.

...

THOUGH MANY OF THE people I interacted with at Sotheby's taxed me greatly, I appreciated the opportunity to learn from each of them. Sotheby's gave me the chance to meet and build relationships with people I would likely never have crossed paths with otherwise. From them, I learned that most people have their insecurities and frailties, as we all do. Being upfront and direct was, by far, the best way to deal with them.

15

The Sotheby's Price-Fixing Scandal

THE SOTHEBY'S PRICE-FIXING SCANDAL HIT the art world in 2001. It nearly brought Sotheby's down and was a tragedy for all those involved. As CEO of Sotheby's for a decade, I had an up-close view of how the company worked, since I had played the major role in rebuilding it. And that included the promotion of Dede Brooks, which ultimately brought the institution to the brink of ruin. The scandal sent Al Taubman to jail, but I am convinced he was the fall guy.

Taubman's reputation was, of course, totally shattered when the jury decided against him in a case that completely stunned the art world. Although our personal relationship had deteriorated somewhat toward the end of my time there, I felt sorry for him. Dede Brooks had insisted under oath that Taubman directed her to meet with Christopher Davidge, the boss of Sotheby's great rival, Christie's, and that he masterminded the illegal price-fixing talks that had taken place.[1] After the trial, she rationalized her actions by telling many people that she had carried out the illegal price fixing to help out the Sotheby's people by improving the stock price. While I can't say for certain since I was not there, I don't believe that Taubman forced Dede to do anything. Clearly my experience with Taubman showed that he never made me do anything I did not feel was proper and appropriate for the company.

...

DEDE BROOKS WAS A mixed blessing and became a real challenge for me. In trying to give rein to her outgoing personality that could be so persuasively good for the company, I had granted her more and more authority over the years. However, after a while, I began to realize she was inclined to make major decisions without discussion or approval.

One such incident occurred on November 11, 1987, which was a historic day for Sotheby's and the art market. On that evening, at a Sotheby's black-tie auction in New York, $53.9 million was paid for Vincent van Gogh's *Irises*. The price was a world record for a work of art and created huge excitement and press interest. Several days later, the art media figured out that the buyer was Alan Bond, an Australian real estate entrepreneur who also owned major media properties. The price set a new standard for the value of great paintings and was not topped until Christie's later sold van Gogh's *Portrait of Dr. Gachet* for $82.5 million in May 1990.[2]

What the press did not know for almost two years was the fact that Bond had bought *Irises* partly on borrowed money. He had paid half of the purchase price in cash, and Sotheby's had financed the other $27 million. When this became public in 1989, a furor ensued.

Geraldine Norman, the aggressive, always skeptical art writer for *The Times* of London, took this on as her cause, alleging that Sotheby's had artificially inflated the art market through the financing of this purchase. Rita Reif, *The New York Times* art writer, became equally vociferous, quoting dealers who claimed the same. Reif quoted Alan E. Salz of the Paris dealership Didier Aaron as saying, "Every painting sold since then has been measured against it." Reif also said that the fact that Sotheby's had stored *Irises* in an undisclosed place had "stirred disquiet."[3]

Behind the scenes, another drama unfolded. As I have noted in the previous chapter, we had a policy at Sotheby's of requiring executive committee approval of any loan greater than $5 million. But the three committee members—Taubman, Max Fisher, and I—only learned of the Alan Bond *Irises* financing after the sale had already occurred. No approval of the financing had been sought from me or, as I learned not long afterward, from Max Fisher. Incensed, I went to Taubman. He brushed it off, making me think that Dede had probably discussed it with him prior to making the offer to Bond, but no one would later own up to what had actually happened.

Geraldine and Rita kept the drums beating over the company's inappropriate use of credit to "jack up prices." Taubman and Dede insisted that we had done nothing wrong, and though they were technically correct in that no law or regulation had been violated, some of our most important clients began to weigh in with criticisms of their own. They were buyers of major works of art and felt they were being forced to pay higher prices because of our offer of financing to some clients. When Leonard Lauder, a major art collector and CEO of Estée Lauder, called me and was quite irate, I began to take serious note, since he was a huge buyer and friend of both Taubman and Sotheby's.

Against the strong advice of Taubman and Dede, I formulated a new policy for our financing activity. It stated that we would "not lend against a work of art until it had been owned by its current owner for at least one year." In this way, we could continue our lending activity on consignments and permanent collections but would stop lending against newly purchased art. Though I received much criticism when I circulated this internally, it was clear to me that this was a measure we needed to take to earn back trust from our major clients. We implemented this policy in 1989, and the issue quickly died down.

The Bond drama continued, however, since he had difficulty settling the debt and finally sold a Manet in 1989 to finish paying for it. The buying and selling of hugely expensive paintings became interwoven in the financial demise of the extravagant Australian entrepreneur. The man who had become an Aussie hero in 1983 when he bankrolled the America's Cup victory, thus inflicting the first-ever defeat on the New York Yacht Club after 132 invincible years, was equally profligate with other acquisitions, such as Australia's Channel Nine TV network, for which he paid A$1.05 billion. When Bond was convicted of fraud and sent to jail for four years in 1992, Kerry Packer, the original Channel Nine owner, bought his network back for a pittance and remarked, "You only get one Alan Bond in your lifetime, and I've had mine."[4]

Remarkably, Bond rebuilt his fortune after his jail term by becoming involved with mining interests in Africa and Madagascar. By 2008, he was named in the *Business Review Weekly* (now *BRW*) "Rich 200 List," with a net worth of $265 million.

Happily for the art world, the *Irises* story had a great ending when, in a sale arranged by Sotheby's, the painting was purchased by the Getty Museum in March 1990, where it hangs today as an icon of their collection.

In retrospect, Dede's violation of our internal policy on gaining prior approval on large financings seemed to follow a pattern I had observed on several occasions. She repeated this pattern with a $105 million loan that never received executive committee approval in 1993.[5] This loan was highlighted in the price-fixing trial as an example of how she dominated Taubman.

Equally interesting was Taubman's grumbling about the new policy eliminating the financing of purchases. He disagreed mightily with me on the policy, as he had earlier on my decisions to stop selling ivory and to hold the auction in Moscow. However, he did not then, nor did he ever, overrule me. In fact, after he got some calls from clients like Lauder, agreeing with the new policy, I think he realized he was wrong, and this was good for Sotheby's.

· · ·

IN 1993, AS I neared the end of my ten-year contract with Taubman, our cost cutting and buyer's premium increases had resulted in a return to good profitability after the 1990–91 art market recession. I had no interest in leaving Sotheby's, but I also had no interest in working any longer with

Taubman and Dede. So quietly, I went to a good friend on Wall Street, Jack Hennessy, CEO of First Boston, to see if we could put together a plan to buy out Taubman. Quickly working with Andy Taussig, one of his top investment bankers, we came up with a plan. Sotheby's stock was trading around thirteen dollars a share at the time. I agreed to put up my two million shares, and we would offer Taubman a 20% premium or sixteen dollars a share for his stock and, if successful, would later do a secondary offering to redistribute the shares.

The weakness in our plan was the absence of leverage over Taubman. Nonetheless, I went to him and made the offer. He was initially surprised but agreed to consider it and did so for a few days. Given how much he loved the spotlight Sotheby's provided him, he came back and said that he would not sell. It was then I told him I would be leaving shortly when my contract was completed.

...

NOTHING HAD A LONGER-TERM impact in all manner of ways than a decision I took regarding Dede Brooks. She had arrived at Sotheby's— when it was still known as Sotheby Parke-Bernet—from Citibank after graduating from Yale. She was tall, with a mane of blonde hair, and turned heads wherever she went, not only because of her looks but also because of the friendly and forceful way in which she presented herself. Dede would never go unnoticed. She was willful and wonderful and, if I had only known it at the time, ultimately dangerous.

In my early days at Sotheby's, I witnessed Dede's talent and instinct for making money. She always had a creative idea on securing consignments from sellers, when competing against Christie's, normally with a new financial "deal," either a loan or a guarantee or a contribution to the seller's charity. Unfortunately, on the next consignment, Christie's would often use a similar approach, and the competitive price war would only get more intense.

Our executive talent was thin. We needed Dede, and I promoted her several times, first to executive vice president of Sotheby's in New York. Later, I made her president of the North American company and invited her (and other senior executives) to sit in on Sotheby's board meetings. It was at these meetings that I saw her "darker" side. She, other senior executives, and I would always meet before board meetings and agree on a management position on the issues. But, in the meetings, I would be dismayed to see that Dede would often break ranks and go her own way.

I was still CEO of Sotheby's when Dede began her "liaison" with Christopher Davidge, the CEO of Christie's. Her collusion was extensive and well documented. At the trial, it came out that Davidge had maintained a treasure trove of documentation chronicling their deliberations, amounting to more than 500 pages of illegal exchanges and agreements.[6] This took place over five years and not only covered agreements on a fixed, nonnegotiable schedule of sellers' commissions but also included lists of clients who would be exclusive to one house or the other and included a detailed agreement on the non-poaching of employees. With these agreements, they guaranteed future profits and clearly showed absolutely no regard for clients or employees of the two firms.

As was proven after exhaustive legal inquiries, I had absolutely no knowledge of their meetings. The only reason I was still even leading Sotheby's at the time she and Davidge began their collusion was because of my own sense of uneasiness about what I'd seen in her. Even Taubman had a reluctance to immediately promote her to the position of CEO as my successor. After he rejected my offer to buy his shares in the fall of 1993, Taubman asked me whom I would recommend as a replacement.

"The only person in the company who can run it is Dede," I told him. "But there is a problem. No one trusts her." She was intensively competitive and often recommended that a client sell a painting in New York when it might have sold for more money at Sotheby's in London or Hong Kong. It was a problem that had been brewing for some time.

Taubman then asked, "Would you stay on for a while and let us see if she can correct that and build some support?" Since I had a strong personal interest in seeing the company do well, I said yes. I suggested that Dede become worldwide chief operating officer, while I remained as CEO, and Taubman agreed.

In this role, she became responsible for all day-to-day auction operations worldwide. She began going to London and Asia on a regular basis, as I had been doing for the past ten years, and within months, she won the Brits and others over with her charm and intensity. So, after a few months, Taubman and I agreed that I would leave and Dede would take over. Little did poor Taubman know that he was signing his path to prison.

I spent a fascinating decade as CEO of this iconic company, and after I handed things over to Dede in 1994, I stayed on the board and on the executive committee of the board with Taubman and Max Fisher. I functioned in this capacity until I fully resigned from the board and sold all my stock in 1996.

A sad parting was the event that prompted my departure. Lucy Mitchell Innes was the strong head of contemporary art worldwide, based in New York, and the only true threat to Dede as CEO. Had I stayed beyond my initial ten years, I would have promoted Lucy to president. In 1996, at a board meeting, I learned that Dede was reassigning Lucy to handle all private sales of art in all departments. This was a new position and not an easy one, since experts are generally only strong in one field. Lucy resigned shortly thereafter. But that was only half of the company's loss. Lucy was married to David Nash, Sotheby's outstanding head of impressionist paintings worldwide. It was only a matter of a few weeks before David resigned as well and, together with Lucy, formed the formidable art-dealing firm of Mitchell-Innes & Nash. Today, they remain a force in both fields, and Sotheby's had lost its two major profit producers.

It was not until the story broke in the *Financial Times* in 2000 that I learned of the price fixing that had occurred years earlier. I had no knowledge of what Dede had been up to with Christopher Davidge and felt betrayed and sickened. I'd devoted a decade of my life to building up Sotheby's, and in finally entrusting the role of CEO to Dede, I had hoped she would rise to the occasion. As I have said, I do not believe Taubman forced her to participate in a Sotheby's-Christie's collusion. In the years since the price fixing became public, I have spoken with many people, including some of Dede's oldest and closest friends, who say that "no one ever *made* Dede do anything." Without a doubt, my experience was that she did things her way.

When legal proceedings began, Dede, to her credit, told the Department of Justice (DOJ) that I knew nothing about the meetings and illegal activity, but that Taubman knew it all and had directed her to carry out the price fixing with Christie's. I saw Dede at a party at some point after the trial and thanked her for being honest with the DOJ. Her declaration did not, however, release me from the need to spend many months convincing investigators that I had no involvement with the scandal.

When the DOJ looked back at the buyer's premium changes I had initiated in 1992, they asked with whom I had discussed these changes before announcing them. I responded honestly that only my wife, my senior management team, and the board had known of the changes. There was one other consultation, that being my YPO forum. (More on my YPO forum in chapter 17.) They learned that my forum was a small group of fellow CEOs who act as a personal board of directors advising each other on important issues and who maintain a complete bond of confidentiality. Interestingly, this helped convince the DOJ that I had not colluded with Christie's, since they observed that no one engaged in illegal activity would have shared sensitive information with such a group.

When the investigations were eventually completed, the DOJ concluded the truth, which I and others had maintained from the start: that I had been completely out of the loop from the whole scandal.

In the end, no one but Dede and Taubman will ever know exactly what happened. I certainly do not, but my strong opinion is that Dede led the way on the collusion. Taubman passed away in 2015 at the age of ninety-one, and his knowledge of the real story went with him.

...

DESPITE THE PROBLEMS THAT were brewing behind the scenes toward the end of my tenure, I can look back on my time at Sotheby's with far more fondness and sense of achievement than regret. In many ways, it was the highlight of my working life. It was thrilling to be involved in selling great art, and, while challenging, the international aspect of running a worldwide organization like Sotheby's was fascinating, educational, and rewarding. I remain grateful for the experience and the many good people I met during those years.

Revamping the USTA

16

Serving in Professional Tennis

BECAME INVOLVED WITH THE UNITED States Tennis Association (USTA) through my friendship with Eugene L. Scott, an omnipresent figure in American tennis who was the US Court Tennis Association champion on ten occasions between 1974–84 and a remarkable athlete.[1] Gene Scott also possessed a serious intellect and, after getting his law degree, began working in the world of tennis, founding his magazine *Tennis Week* in the mid-1970s. His editorials, which tested the reach of one's vocabulary and provoked arguments, became a must-read for the tennis community. Due to his intellect and great tennis knowledge, he became an advisor to young tennis talent on the East Coast, players like John McEnroe, Vitas Gerulaitis, and a whole host of others. Gene was a regular member of our tennis group at the River Club in New York City. I tried to hold my own in our weekly doubles matches, which often involved Gene, the great South African tennis pro Owen Williams, and my wife, Suzanne, who was far closer in ability to these former tour players than I was.

Gene ran tournaments at South Orange, New Jersey, and, later, at the Rye Town Hilton in Westchester County before being appointed tournament director for the ATP Masters at Madison Square Garden. In 1989, a Russian entrepreneur called Sasson Khakshouri arrived in New York and told Gene he wanted to start a big tournament in Moscow. After observing

Gene's work for a few days, Khakshouri asked him if he would run it for him. Taking the plunge, Gene took some of his *Tennis Week* staff with him and set up shop at the vast Olympic Stadium in Moscow with a remit to find a $1 million sponsorship in nine months. Boris Yeltsin had just become the Russian president, and the fact that he was a tennis fanatic helped smooth Gene's path. Nevertheless, it took some ingenuity on the part of this non-Russian-speaking New Yorker, and when he got Bayer on board, the Kremlin Cup was launched and immediately became one of the best attended tournaments on the ATP Tour. At Gene's invitation, I went to Moscow in 1991 to speak at a business leaders conference Gene put on in conjunction with the Kremlin Cup.

In 1992, Gene asked Suzanne and me if we could do something about the International Tennis Hall of Fame's gala dinner. The gala had a great position on the Friday night of finals week of the US Open, but the event had become a bit lackluster in recent years. We agreed to help and began by moving the dinner to the Waldorf Astoria, shortening the presentation ceremonies, augmenting the introduction of the new inductees with video footage of their achievements, and bringing in some musical entertainment. We jazzed it up in order to create a fun evening and ramped up the fundraising from the gala.

Around this time, I started meeting many of the tennis hierarchy, including the hall of fame's executive committee chairman John Reese of Lazard Frères & Co. John had taken over from the legendary Joe Cullman of Philip Morris, whose energy and financial support had done so much to build the International Tennis Hall of Fame at the remarkable historic Newport Casino with its ten outdoor grass tennis courts in Newport, Rhode Island.

By chance, Suzanne and I happened to have Pierce O'Neil, the USTA's chief business officer, as a neighbor in Connecticut where we both had homes. We became friends and tennis partners over the years. One day, Pierce asked me if I would be interested in having my name put forward for the USTA board. I had just finished my tenure at Sotheby's and had a little more time on my hands, despite already spending several hours a week working with The Posse Foundation. I said yes to Pierce and was elected to the board in 1997.

...

THE USTA WAS A hugely profitable organization, with the US Open, one of the biggest sporting events in the world, generating an annual surplus, when I joined the board, of about $100 million. These funds were then parceled out to the seventeen sections that ran the many programs of the USTA, many of which were most worthwhile and truly did "Grow the Game," as its slogan read. Though the USTA had enjoyed remarkable growth over the years, mainly through the revenue generated from the US Open, it was an organization that faced many problems. I quickly discovered that this was no ordinary board. It was a group of about thirty people who, for all intents and purposes, were running the USTA from top to bottom, including the US Open. I could see that they were functioning like an operating committee, not a board.

Had I realized how much time was required to be a USTA board member, I might have originally balked at the idea. The board, I came to realize, met almost every month, and the meetings were not brief. They started on Thursday and ended a few days later on Sunday afternoons. During the meetings, board members got into the minutiae of the organization's day-to-day affairs in a way that would never have been considered appropriate for a regular company board, and given my experience, I thought it frustrating and dysfunctional, not to mention time consuming. In checking my board responsibilities against my schedule, I later found that I had been involved with USTA matters, either in person or for two- to three-hour-long phone calls, for a total of 150 days in a calendar year.

There was a personal problem too because, by chance and unbeknownst to me, I ended up replacing Gene on the board. Gene had been edged out after people felt he was using his position to get preferential treatment for the location and size of his *Tennis Week* booth at the US Open. Many objected to the frankness of his *Tennis Week* editorials, some of which were critical of the USTA. There was no question that Gene had used his ability to sell seats to sponsors out of his courtside box as a financial lifeline because *Tennis Week*, despite its respected position in the game, never made money. Unfortunately, the fact that I had taken his spot on the board soured our friendship a bit, which was a shame.

Gene's departure was unfortunate for the USTA too because he was hugely more qualified to help guide the association's fortunes than some of the small-town businesspeople, professors, and teachers who were working their way assiduously toward the presidency. The whole thing was incredibly political with the geographic sections jostling for position and jobs, and I must admit that, in this instance, my attempts to change the culture of the board failed.

I quickly identified some like-minded people on the board who shared a vision for improving things and moving the organization forward. These included individuals like Judy Levering, who would become the USTA's first-ever female president in 1999 when she succeeded Harry Marmion; Alan Schwartz, a tennis entrepreneur from Chicago; and Pam Shriver, the former US Open finalist, who became a great friend and ally as we tried to professionalize some of the management decisions. Pam and I believed that the board could function more effectively.

We did get as far as bringing in McKinsey & Company to study the way the USTA worked, but with too many vested interests among board members, I could see that no one truly wanted change. When McKinsey made the necessary proposals, they were all voted down. The vote, I recall, wasn't even close, and there were no more than three or four people who voted as I did. Also, the fact that we'd voted by secret ballot demonstrated to me how fearful board members were of showing their reactionary tendencies. Interestingly, I learned that the same thing had happened ten years earlier when McKinsey was brought in to help; the proposals went nowhere, and McKinsey was shown the door.

So I proceeded the best I could.

...

I CAME TO UNDERSTAND that on the board of the USTA, the president, an amateur official elected for a period of just two years, also served as the chairman, CEO, and tournament director of the US Open. I was a leading member of a group on the board who realized that inexperienced, short-term amateur leadership with rotating presidents wasn't going to keep getting the job done. When Judy Levering came to me just before she took over as president and said, "Michael, I'm going to be running this huge event, and I don't have a clue," it was obvious to me that we needed to hire a top professional. Judy and I did some heavy lobbying to get the USTA board to agree. Many feared they might lose some power should they later head the USTA. In the end, the board decided to hire two—one to run the US Open and professional tennis and one to take care of community tennis—to help us manage both the professional and amateur arms of the USTA.

We put a headhunter to work and were given the name of Arlen Kantarian, a former marketing chief at the NFL, who was then running Radio City Music Hall in Manhattan. One of Arlen's biggest assets, apart from an outgoing, can-do type of personality, was his experience in dealing with TV networks. I was asked to negotiate his contract and, after consultation with the board, offered him a bonus if he could accelerate the surplus above the 6% rate at which US Open net revenue was growing each year. We decided to give him 10% of that surplus so that the USTA would get the first 6% and 90% of the rest. As anyone who has followed the fortunes of the championships will know, Arlen did a fabulous job and, after only five years, ended up pocketing an incredible $9 million. Though, during that time, the US Open became an even bigger gold mine for the USTA, the board was reluctant to let him get any richer, so sadly, that relationship ended in 2008. It was, in my opinion, a shortsighted decision by the board.

All the same, Arlen had brought about numerous positive changes to the US Open over the years. For a start, he moved the women's final away from what used to be known as Super Saturday, where it was sandwiched between the two men's semifinals, to its own spot on Friday evening. That brought in more revenue through ticket prices and a much heightened profile and expanded sponsorship for the women's game.

Arlen also took away the courtside photographers' pit on the south side of Arthur Ashe Stadium and turned it into luxury boxes, which brought in a ton of money.

His most expansive idea, based on his knowledge of the way television executives' minds work, was the creation of the US Open Series, which benefited the game far beyond the confines of the US Open. By working with the ATP and WTA, who run their individual tours separate from the Grand Slams, Arlen linked all the tour events staged in America and Canada during the weeks prior to the US Open by creating a point system. The players earning the most points from winning these North American events, which would all be televised by CBS or ESPN, would be rewarded with extra prize money. And this prize money was not exactly peanuts. The men's and women's winner of the US Open Series would double their winnings if they also won the US Open, and even if they didn't, they would still take home a nice chunk of change.

In 2014, Serena Williams created a record for the total amount of money earned by a woman at one sporting event by winning $4 million, between her prize money for winning the US Open and for having finished first in the US Open Series.[2] In the previous year, Serena and Rafael Nadal had each earned $3.6 million.[3]

Arlen's idea was also extremely popular with the tournament directors because it provided a major incentive for top names to play some of the smaller events that they might otherwise bypass with the US Open looming.

• • •

MEANWHILE, BECAUSE I CAME from the art world, I was asked to chair a committee that was tasked with the job of creating a suitable memorial for tennis legend Arthur Ashe. Though the naming of the stadium had been a wonderful and deserving honor, nothing on the grounds of the Billie Jean King National Tennis Center explained why Ashe's name had been attached to the vast edifice that greets visitors as they walk through the gates.

I agreed to take on the job as long as Arthur's widow, the beautiful and charming photographer Jeannie Moutoussamy-Ashe, would work with me and co-chair the project. When she agreed, we asked the great photographer Gordon Parks, whose photo books Jeannie had read as a child in Chicago, and Ray Nasher, a renowned collector of sculptures in Dallas, to join us on the selection committee with a couple of others. We also hired Nancy Rosen Blackwood as an art consultant. She had achieved notoriety in selecting all the art for the Disney cruise ships, among other assignments.

The selection committee decided to create a competition for artists to offer their ideas for a sculpture that would stand just inside the entrance to the South Gate and opposite the fountains. The brief we created told artists to give vent to their imaginations and not be tied down to too tight a definition of Arthur Ashe, the tennis player.

We had about twenty responses, among which was some fairly phantasmagorical stuff, but our committee was most taken by a work created by Eric Fischl, a painter and sculptor who was known for his challenging and sometimes disturbing art. He lived on Long Island, enjoyed playing tennis, and was a good friend of John McEnroe, who had opened his own art gallery in Manhattan some years before. As a sculptor, Fischl was a disciple of Rodin, and his offering was a fifteen-foot bronze statue of a powerful nude male, rising out of a mound of earth, seemingly in the act of serving a tennis ball. It was heroic, aspirational, subtle, and symbolic. It was not Arthur but a rendering of what he stood for.

It was also clearly too progressive for some members of the USTA board. But Alan Schwartz and Judy Levering loved it as much as our committee did. This helped when, with much trepidation, I took a two-foot version of the sculpture to the board for their perusal. The nudity was one of the main issues the board had with it, and much was made of the need for the genitalia to be extremely subtle. I mentioned this to Eric, and he said, "Oh, don't worry. It will be just a thumbprint."

Initially, this did not turn out to be the case. When I went to have a look at an all-white half-size cast in Eric's studio, a side-on view clearly revealed the outline of a flaccid penis. To me, the thumb had obviously not done its work. After Eric received my feedback that he needed to tone it down, he promised to do so, and there was little hint of genitalia on the finished sculpture.

Michael Ainslie with artist Eric Fischl in his workshop with the fifteen-foot bronze statue before installation as the Arthur Ashe Memorial at the US Open stadium, spring 2002.

Penis resizing proved less time-consuming than raising the money for the project, although I did manage to achieve that faster than anyone imagined I would. We had been told that the entire project—the bronze sculpture, as well as the landscaping of the garden around it by Mark Sullivan of Paul Friedberg Associates—would cost $1 million, but even Alan Schwartz looked a little dubious when I said I was going to raise the money through contributions.

It didn't turn out to be too much trouble. I sent out one hundred letters to friends from the tennis world and other likely candidates, asking them for gifts of $25,000 to commemorate Arthur Ashe in fitting style, on receipt of which the donor would receive a twenty-four-inch numbered miniature of Fischl's work cast in bronze and his or her name at the base of the sculpture. Forty people took up the offer, thus quickly providing us with the required $1 million. To show our thanks, we also gave them all a lunch at the 21 Club, a legendary restaurant in Manhattan, to show off Fischl's creation.

I think some members of the USTA were amazed that we had pulled it off. The work itself certainly created controversy, but Jeanne Moutous-samy-Ashe loved it, which was what mattered most.

For me, some years after the sculpture was unveiled, it was particularly gratifying when those who had previously criticized the statue expressed that they had grown to understand and admire it. It was also well received by David Dinkins, the former mayor of New York, who is a real tennis person and a most charming and discerning man.[4] Dinkins, in his first year of office in 1990, persuaded Air Traffic Control at LaGuardia to nudge the flight path of the jets a little bit to the east or west of the tennis center during the tournament, allowing for a marked improvement in the experience of tennis fans. Prior to that, planes had roared over Louis Armstrong Stadium at frighteningly low altitudes every ninety seconds, which was more than a little distracting for players and spectators alike.[5]

Once the controversy over the statue died down and people stopped asking, "Where are the shorts?" I think the result worked out well. Spectators arriving at the South Gate of the United States Tennis Center now enter along the Champions' Walk—a Judy Levering concept—which features photographs and bios of US Open champions and then arrive at the little garden with its imposing sculpture and a marble panel telling Ashe's life story. I'd asked my late brother Peter Ainslie, a talented writer, to research and write the text for the story, which would be enshrined in marble at the base of the statue. He did so eloquently, even including important words from Ashe such as, "From what we get, we can make a living; what we give, however, makes a life." That was typical of Ashe's thinking, and I was proud to have played a role in creating a proper memorial to a truly important world figure.

...

MIDWAY THROUGH HER TERM, in 2000, Judy Levering asked me if I would follow her and stand for the USTA presidency. I first asked Judy how much of the year she was giving to the USTA with the required attendance at the four Grand Slams, the Davis Cup, and Fed Cup trips abroad, and the endless meetings. She replied that it was more than 300 days a year. But I had agreed to partner with my wife, Suzanne, to raise our daughter, Serena, who was only two years old at the time. The presidency would have been an honor, quite apart from the nice perks that came with the position, such as two seats in the USTA president's box for life. After much deliberation with Suzanne, and having failed to change the culture of the USTA despite my best efforts, I declined Judy's offer, eventually rotating off the board altogether. In retrospect, it was the right decision for us.

I enjoyed a wonderful decade in professional tennis and value the friendships I made with people like Judy, Arlen Kantarian, Alan Schwartz, Pierce O'Neil, and Pam Shriver, as well as Patrick McEnroe, who also joined us on the USTA board and later became USTA head of player development. Patrick was a delight and always asked the most insightful questions as he learned more and more about how boards function.

Clearly, the entrepreneurial leadership of Arlen Kantarian, supported by Judy Levering and Alan Schwartz, dramatically improved the profitability of the US Open. This is symbolized by the fact that Arthur Ashe Stadium now has a new roof and a $500 million expansion program just completed. The improved cash flow resulting from the many changes put in by Arlen made it possible to issue the hundreds of millions in tax-free bonds that put a roof over the Ashe stadium, built a new covered Louis Armstrong stadium, allowed for a new Chase corporate entertaining facility, and generally upgraded the Billie Jean King National Tennis Center to its status as the leading tennis facility in the world. These changes would not have been possible without the increased profitability resulting from our efforts, led by Arlen, to professionalize the management of the US Open.

The Lehman Collapse

17

An Inside View

WHEN LEHMAN BROTHERS FILED FOR bankruptcy on September 15, 2008, a global financial catastrophe ensued. As one of the world's biggest and most successful banks, Lehman was a major player not only in the United States but also internationally. This largest bankruptcy filing in history shook market confidence, intensified the 2008 financial crisis, and continues to impact the economy today. Though world markets have learned a lot from the collapse and the mistakes that were made at the time, I still consider this event as one of the toughest moments in my personal and professional life. I saw what happened firsthand. I was there on the night of the vote for bankruptcy. I experienced the fallout afterward. And I maintain, to this day, that the Lehman collapse was a catastrophe that could have been avoided.

...

DICK FULD, THE CHAIRMAN and CEO of Lehman Brothers, assumed control of the company in 1995 when it was struggling as a weak and undercapitalized spin-off from American Express. Fuld, a fierce and driven competitor in the financial world who had earned the tag "Gorilla of Wall Street," put his heart and soul, as well as his money, into the company.

He took the heat when Lehman collapsed and probably lost much of his $1 billion fortune. He was a leader who believed in Lehman so much that he even bought shares on the margin while turning it into a powerhouse.[1]

It is also worth noting that much of the compensation of all Lehman staff was in the form of stock, which did not fully vest for five years. At the time of the bankruptcy, senior management had sizeable holdings in Lehman stock that became worthless. So ultimately Dick Fuld and many others paid dearly for the Lehman collapse.

We all did. During my tenure, none of the board members sold our shares, which was unusual for a board like ours. Dick Fuld believed in the company, and we believed in him. His staff loved the role of underdog and continually brought new clients to the firm. I found him good to work with. He was tough, candid, and open, especially at the dinners that were held on the eve of most every board meeting. They were working dinners in the strictest sense, and although levity was at a premium during these dinners, they helped us bond. Fuld never had a glass of wine. His focus was always on the business of Lehman Brothers.

I got the impression that only two things truly mattered to him—the company and his family. He was a family man to his core and spent all his off-duty hours, such as they were, with his wife and three children. The rest of the time he devoted to Lehman.

His "One firm—we're all in this together" philosophy was influenced by John Macomber, our lead director, who had spent a long period of his career at McKinsey & Company, the management consulting firm where I had worked when I was starting out in my career. It was a McKinsey philosophy I knew well and lived by. Fuld, encouraged by Macomber, cemented this philosophy into the Lehman Brothers business structure, even to the extent of paying his five or six direct reports identically so that they would always feel as if they were working as a team rather than trying to outdo one another. It enabled Fuld to build a culture that strengthened the quality of the firm, as talent was spread around to improve weaker units. Lehman had a history as a strong fixed-income house, but it took some hard work and the sharing of skills to build up equities, research, real estate, investment banking, and many other parts of the firm.

Lehman's culture was strong and combative. It was tough to be the small guy on the street. Some believed that Fuld had Goldman envy, but I would say he was simply determined to outcompete Goldman Sachs. Later, when warning lights started flashing for Lehman, Fuld was slow to embrace the idea of merging with another company for fear of losing the culture he had so carefully and intentionally built. But this was an expensive mistake and might have been the beginning of the end for his company.

After Lehman's fall, I presume he was sleeping as badly as I was. Inevitably, especially with something as big as this, you can't help but to look at yourself and start asking questions. There were so many questions to ask, so many what-ifs. I wasn't into pinpointing blame, but I'm sure my fellow board members were asking many of the same questions. I wanted to know if something could have been done differently, if there was something more I could have noticed to help avert the fateful sequence of events.

Should we as the board have challenged Joe Gregory's appointment as president of Lehman, for example? In 2004, Fuld, under board pressure to name a number two, had pushed Gregory's appointment through. We know that today, the best board practice would call for a CEO to nominate two or three different candidates for the board to evaluate before it selected one. But this was at a time when Lehman was doing extremely well, and it would have been difficult for us to say no to a CEO who was on the growth path that Fuld had carved out for Lehman. Perhaps we shouldn't have allowed the appointment, but who could have known what would happen? In hindsight, Gregory had a similar set of career experiences at Lehman to Fuld, and they thought alike; this is rarely a good combination for the top two in senior management.

Also, would there have been a better choice, another strong Lehman senior executive who might have slowed the heavy concentration of investments in large, illiquid real estate deals?

And should the board have attempted to stop Lehman's investment in Archstone, the huge $22 billion real estate deal that wound up being the final straw in illiquidity?

Could we have pushed harder for Fuld to find a merger partner with whom to do a deal?

Had our appetite for risk somehow been too high? Or was the value at risk (VAR) bar, which was supposed to act as a barrier in the event of trouble, put too low? Had we been too trusting in risk formulas that had never been fully tested in the kind of market meltdown we saw in 2008?

These were the questions that kept me awake at night, and even now, I am not sure of the answers. In hindsight, Lehman was overleveraged, like every one of our banking and investment banking competitors. But that was not a crime. All our actions and methods of doing business had always been under intense scrutiny, and in fact, we had US Securities and Exchange Commission (SEC) staff working full time in our offices, overseeing, monitoring, and reviewing everything we did. There were no secrets, we had nothing to hide, and no one was doing anything illegal. We realized later that it was just that everyone's crystal ball was cloudy.

Lehman was far from alone in failing to predict the extent of the coming storm. In March 2007, Ben Bernanke, chairman of the Federal Reserve, had this to say while addressing a congressional Joint Economic Committee: "The impact on the broader economy and financial markets of the problems in the subprime market seems likely to be contained."[2] Yet within five months, the $2 trillion subprime market was coming apart at the seams. Bear Stearns was the first to go. In August 2007, investors lost $1.6 billion when the subprime bets that two of its hedge funds had made failed. BNP Paribas, France's largest bank, was also in trouble and admitted an inability to properly price its subprime bonds.

Suddenly, everything seemed too complicated. Experienced financiers and bankers couldn't work out what was what. As Andrew Ross Sorkin wrote in his classic and amazingly detailed book *Too Big to Fail*, "Wall Street was undone by its own smarts . . . almost no one was able to figure out how to price [mortgage-backed securities] in a declining market . . . Without a price the market was paralyzed. And without access to capital, Wall Street simply could not function."[3]

Inevitably, there were a lot of false rumors flying around. But in fact, Lehman's problem was not subprime mortgages. We had small positions in that market, despite what bloggers have put up on the internet post-bankruptcy. Lehman had simply invested too much of its capital in real estate—commercial, residential, raw land, all of it. These assets recovered much of their value over time, but the Federal Reserve's decision to keep Lehman from becoming a bank holding company made these illiquid assets, which we could not use as collateral for borrowing. So it was true that Lehman had a liquidity crisis—we needed cash. But we didn't have a giant equity hole, or an "asset hole," as our competitor CEOs claimed. We had equity—it was depressed, but it was there.

At the time, even with red flags waving, most of us refused to contemplate the magnitude of the oncoming crisis. There is no question that Fuld should have been more aggressive in searching for a partner for Lehman. There had been contact with PaineWebber and, among others, Bank of America, but nothing came out of those discussions. Because Fuld had molded Lehman and carefully created a strong culture, he was afraid it would be weakened or even destroyed if he had to take on the wrong partner. Although I believe he was rightly proud of what he had produced, it might also have blinded his judgment to a certain extent when the walls began to crumble.

Other competitors moved faster. Merrill Lynch was saved on the final weekend by merging with Bank of America. When the writing on the wall was so clear that even Fuld could not ignore it, serious efforts were made to do a deal with Barclays, but, as I have explained, we were thwarted by the refusal of the UK government to grant us a waiver, meaning we would run out of time before anything could be done to save us. In the end, time was our worst enemy—along with Henry Paulson.

...

I BELIEVE HENRY PAULSON, the US secretary of the treasury at the time, panicked. I am not suggesting there wasn't good reason for a bit of panic, because it was clear, over that desperate weekend in September, that many of the world's great financial institutions were teetering on the edge of chaos. Lehman was one of them, but there was also the giant AIG and with it Goldman Sachs. Two others, Morgan Stanley and Merrill Lynch, were not far behind. They were so close, in fact, that a friend who was a board member of Morgan Stanley stated that had Mitsubishi UFJ Financial Group not come through with a $9 billion investment, they would have been right behind us in bankruptcy.

Paulson was a former CEO of Goldman Sachs, where he had made his career and his fortune. He had been reluctant to take the Treasury job and needed to be cajoled and almost even bullied into joining the George W. Bush administration. Paulson was also referred to as "the Reluctant Nominee." He found the confirmation process unpleasant, saying, "If I could have had a do-over, I would have gone right back to C.E.O. of Goldman Sachs."[4] Many of us believed that his heart was still with Goldman Sachs, even after he sold his $480 million worth of Goldman stock. The closeness of his relationship with his successor at Goldman, Lloyd Blankfein, was revealed in a 2009 article written by Andrew Clark, the Wall Street correspondent for *The Guardian*. In his article, Clark stated that during the five or six days covering the weekend of Lehman's bankruptcy and the days that followed, Paulson spoke with Blankfein more than two dozen times, including no fewer than five times on September 17.[5]

Why? Because Goldman was intimately tied to everything that was happening with the crisis at AIG. AIG owed Goldman huge amounts of money, and many believe that Paulson's decision to save AIG while letting Lehman collapse seems rooted in three things:[6]

1. A fear that, if AIG went under, it would drag Goldman with it

2. A fear that Congress would never agree to bail out AIG if he had allowed Lehman to survive

3. A long and difficult relationship with Dick Fuld

This was borne out by the fact that, once the Treasury had given AIG a taxpayer investment (I refuse to call it a "bailout," since the full amount was repaid with a profit to the US government of $22 billion)[7] of $182.5 billion following the Lehman bankruptcy,[8] Goldman Sachs received $12.9 billion from AIG in the form of collateral and cash.[9]

In the same *Guardian* article, Andrew Clark wrote, "Goldman had more at stake than anybody else in seeing that AIG survived. . . . Although Goldman hotly rejects this, [critics contended] that Goldman could have crumbled if [AIG] had failed to cough up its dues. There is no doubt that the treasury's decision to rescue AIG worked hugely in Goldman's favour."[10] Nothing that has been revealed since then contradicts this assumption, so we get down to the question of the personal judgment of Paulson, the man in charge, and his personal relationships with the executives involved.

Paulson was clearly on excellent terms with Blankfein, whereas his relationship with Fuld could best be described as contentious. Paulson felt that Fuld had not tried hard enough to find a partner that could offer an equity infusion. Fuld and Paulson had an earlier conflict when Fuld was asked to have Lehman put money into the collective effort to save Long Term Capital Management. Paulson was leading this effort in 1998 and had Goldman put in $300 million. Lehman was asked to invest $250 million but only put in $100 million, angering Paulson with this participation.[11]

Another insight into the tension between Fuld and Paulson might be drawn from a conversation I had with Robert Steel, then the vice chairman of Goldman Sachs, a few years earlier in August 2006 when we were at a golf clinic in Aspen, Colorado. Steel commented on the great job Fuld had done in building up Lehman in recent years. With Paulson's own deputy giving such compliments, it is hard to imagine that a bit of rivalry, if not outright resentment, didn't exist between the two.

Perhaps an even more revealing comment came from a Goldman executive who departed Goldman in 2004 to manage assets for private clients. With typical Goldman arrogance, he told me over dinner in Palm Beach one evening, "We did not like those Lehman guys. They tried to copy everything we did but weren't good enough to pull it off." I knew there was certainly no love lost between Goldman and Lehman.

For me, and I think many other people, the lingering question that remains is this: Why was Lehman not allowed to become a bank holding company if our competitors—Goldman Sachs, Morgan Stanley, and Merrill Lynch—were given bank holding company status by the secretary of the treasury only days after Lehman was forced into bankruptcy? A bank that is granted bank holding company status is immediately allowed to borrow against its less liquid assets. An alternative would have been to allow Lehman to borrow under the Fed's Primary Dealer Credit Facility (PDCF) that loaned to our competitors. If the federal government had been willing to provide the financing to us, the crisis could have been prevented for a time. It might not have saved Lehman in the long term, but it would have avoided the bankruptcy and saved billions of dollars. What troubles me is that Lehman had been requesting bank holding company status at the same time that approval must have already been in the works for the other three. Tom Russo, Lehman Brothers general counsel, recalls asking Tim Geithner, then president of the New York Fed, about Lehman becoming a bank holding company in the summer of 2008. Geithner disagreed with this idea, arguing that "it would send the wrong signal."[12] However, after Lehman was let go, Goldman Sachs and Morgan Stanley became bank holding companies, thanks to the government.

The fact that Lehman was treated differently than the others looked to be willful on the part of Henry Paulson and Ben Bernanke at the Federal Reserve. Dr. Laurence Ball stated on September 3, 2018, in an article in *The Guardian*,

"Many emails and memos document the discussions among Fed and Treasury officials in the days before the bankruptcy, and they make it clear that the discussions had nothing to do with the Fed's legal authority or Lehman's collateral. Instead, Lehman's fate was determined by officials' views of the political and economic consequences of a Lehman rescue or a Lehman bankruptcy. The deciding factor was politics: the decision-makers, especially Paulson, were unwilling to endure the intense criticism that would have followed a Lehman rescue. Having experienced the backlash from politicians and the media against the Fed's loan to Bear Stearns in March 2008 and the government takeovers of Fannie Mae and Freddie Mac in early September, Paulson told the others: 'I can't do it again. I can't be Mr Bailout.' Paulson's chief of staff put the point bluntly in an email to Paulson's press secretary: 'I just can't stomach us bailing out Lehman . . . will look horrible in the press, don't u think?'"[13]

Regarding the collateral issue, Ball continues in the same *Guardian* article "If one examines Lehman's finances on the eve of its bankruptcy, it is clear that the firm did have ample collateral to borrow the cash it needed to stay in business, a fact that officials would have discovered had they actually looked."[14]

Although in a February 21, 2014, *New York Times* report by Peter Eavis, Bernanke was quoted as saying, "'The Fed and Treasury simply had no tools to address both Lehman and the other companies that were under stress at that time.'"[15] I had an inside view of things, and I know this was simply not true. A more accurate statement would have admitted that they found the tools—offering bank holding status—for the others but not for Lehman. As Eavis pointed out in a March 2008 piece, the Federal Reserve had "found the tools to bail out Bear Stearns, another Wall Street firm toppling under the weight of soured [subprime] mortgages."[16]

Tom Russo, Lehman's general counsel, spoke in September 2016 at the NYU Law and Management of Financial Service Businesses program and stated, "I first heard the government's rationale about a lack of legal power from the Federal Reserve Chairman Ben Bernanke in a speech on October 15, 2008, at the Economic Club of New York. I found it hard to believe since up to that point I had taken the then Treasury Secretary Hank Paulson's reported words as gospel—he 'never once considered that it was appropriate to put taxpayer money on the line . . . in resolving Lehman Brothers.' If he never considered such a move, how did concerns about legal power enter the conversation? Questions about the legality of a bailout would have been moot, as the government never intended to provide one."[17]

In *The Financial Crisis Inquiry Report*, John Thain, the former chairman of Merrill Lynch who arranged its sale to Bank of America, is quoted as saying, "'There was never discussion to the best of my recollection that [the Fed] couldn't [bail out Lehman]. It was only that they wouldn't.'"[18]

Dick Fuld continued to insist that regulators had used "flawed information" in denying Lehman aid. Lehman filed for bankruptcy with $639 billion in assets.[19] To the person on the street, this must have seemed absurd. And financial experts from around the world were quick to criticize the way Lehman had been allowed to fail. "'For the equilibrium of the world financial system, this was a genuine error,'" said Christine Lagarde, who was the French finance minister at the time.[20]

This was a tragedy for so many people, but it could have been prevented. Lehman didn't have to collapse in the way that it did, wreaking havoc on the world economy. And Paulson has still never answered the question "why one and not the other?" over offering bank holding status.

. . .

I HAD ONE FACE-TO-FACE encounter with Henry Paulson before the Lehman crisis. For many years, I was a member of the Young Presidents Organization, better known as YPO. Most YPO members joined a forum of twelve or fourteen CEOs. My forum met regularly and functioned like a personal board of directors.[21] In addition to monthly meetings, annual retreats were held by my forum to discuss various macro topics, and it was during one of these retreats in the fall of 2007 that I led the group down to Washington, DC, to meet with leading government officials. We met with Vice President Dick Cheney, Senator Lamar Alexander, Ambassador Dennis Ross, and others to get their views on the upcoming 2008 election, the Middle East, and other important topics. We also met with Henry Paulson. Paulson arrived with his undersecretary, Robert Steel, whom I mentioned before and who had followed Paulson from Goldman Sachs to the Treasury.

I found Paulson not very verbal and somewhat ponderous in his delivery, but I remember being impressed with what he told us about his efforts to use the power of the Treasury to go after international banks holding terrorists' accounts around the world. He was intent on rounding up this cash and stemming the flow of money between terrorist organizations. I saw that he was trying to use the power of his office in a creative way, putting his experience in global financial markets to good use, and he came across as savvy and committed to me. This only increased my disappointment and frustration when, some eighteen months later, he failed to be either creative or committed to the daunting task of saving the world's economies from the incredible pain that ensued from the Lehman collapse.

And these sentiments only increased when I learned that HBO invited Paulson into the editing room for the movie version of *Too Big to Fail*, covering the events of September 2008. I was astounded that anyone so deeply involved with the outcome of these controversial events should be asked to help write their history. Though I made my concerns known by calling a contact on the editorial board of *The Wall Street Journal*, sadly, they did nothing. I imagine they called HBO and were told HBO had just been fact-checking with Paulson. But my sources tell me he had a far more active role than fact-checking. My worst fears were realized when Paulson came out in the movie as the hero. Almost inevitably, considering the influence he had during the filming, HBO's *Too Big to Fail* makes him look like God.

Paulson was definitely not that, and I will leave it to others to decide how far he fell from grace in not helping those who could have been helped.

18

The Truth of the Matter

O N THAT FINAL WEEKEND LEADING up to the bankruptcy, there was nothing more galling, more frustrating, or more ridiculous than the news that Henry Paulson and the succeeding secretary of the treasury, Tim Geithner, had hauled the CEOs of all of Lehman Brothers' biggest competitors down to the New York Federal Reserve building to work out a way of saving our necks. The fact that none of the CEOs had the slightest incentive to want to save a tough competitor only underlined the state of near panic that was gripping everyone in the financial world and beyond. In *Lehman Brothers: A Crisis of Value*, author Oonagh McDonald writes, "Paulson now acknowledges, as some in the room suspected, that the government was more amenable to funding a rescue than it let on." Paulson explained, " 'We said, "No public money." . . . We said this publicly. We repeated it when these guys came in. But to ourselves we said, "If there's a chance to put in public money and avert a disaster, we're open to it." ' "[1]

If one had wanted to create a theater of the absurd, this would have been a good way to do it. The directors were Paulson and Geithner, and they were telling the actors to come up with their own lines.

On that Saturday morning, the bank CEOs were arranged in working groups: Citigroup, Merrill Lynch, and Morgan Stanley were put in charge of analyzing Lehman's balance sheet and liquidity issues. Goldman Sachs,

Credit Suisse, and Deutsche Bank were to study our real estate assets and determine the size of the equity hole. According to Andrew Ross Sorkin in *Too Big to Fail*, Geithner told the startled group, "'As you know, the government's not doing this, you're on your own, figure it out, make it happen. . . . I'm going to come back in two hours; you guys better figure out a solution and get this thing done.'"[2] In two hours? Save Lehman Brothers and with it the financial economy as we knew it? In two hours? As Sorkin wrote, "His tone struck the many in room as patronizing if not ridiculous. 'This is fucking nuts,'" Sorkin quoted Vikram Pandit of Citigroup as saying to John Mack of Morgan Stanley.[3]

We know the results. The CEOs did not come up with a means of saving Lehman from going under. But that did not prevent Kenneth Lewis of Bank of America and John Thain of Merrill Lynch from working out a deal that weekend, whereby Bank of America bought Merrill for $50 billion.

. . .

AFTER THE COLLAPSE, ONE of the challenges faced by the court was to reconstruct Lehman to determine what had really caused the bankruptcy. Judge James M. Peck, the bankruptcy judge, appointed Anton Valukas, a partner in the Chicago law firm of Jenner & Block, as the bankruptcy examiner. Valukas was deemed to be an independent and objective lawyer capable of figuring out what had happened to Lehman, including the events that led up to its downfall.

Valukas and his team produced a bankruptcy examiner report, which ended up being 2,200 pages long. The work took more than a year and cost, believe it or not, about $100 million. It included scores of lawyers and forensic accountants trawling through every detail to determine if there had been evidence of fraud. They came to many conclusions, the most important of which was that Lehman was solvent until five days before the bankruptcy.

Another conclusion was that Lehman had a "run on the bank," during which clients began pulling their accounts and funds, and hedge funds were shorting the Lehman stock. CNBC fed the fears, as a reporter named Charlie Gasparino seemed intent on airing every possible negative opinion on Lehman.

As a result of his research, Valukas found, to use the technical term, no "colorable claims" against the board. He determined that the Lehman board had continued to carry out its fiduciary duties. Had he concluded otherwise, the examiner's report would have become a road map for shareholders and bondholders to sue, and both directors and management would have been in serious legal and personal financial trouble.

Further, not everyone was happy with the fact that Lehman's management had used a technique called Repo 105 to modestly deleverage the balance sheet. Some critics called it a trick, whereby you could sell assets at the end of a quarter and buy them back in the next quarter. Although permission to use Repo 105 was never brought to the board, it was apparently a widely used and accepted practice, accepted by the SEC, and authorized by our lawyers and auditors. In a 2010 survey, *The Wall Street Journal* found that every major bank and investment bank utilized Repo 105. This was a practice, however, that was disallowed after the 2008 meltdown, an example of closing the barn door a little too late.[4]

Valukas concluded that Lehman's daily mark-to-market procedure had been followed correctly and that Lehman had been writing down its assets in a reasonable manner as the crisis developed. He found only two areas where he felt the marks were not accurate. One was the subprime inventory, which he thought was marked down too far, believe it or not. And the other was the $35 billion of commercial real estate, which he considered was not marked down far enough but only by a total of $3 billion, or about 10%.

Valukas reviewed thirty-four million pages of documentation, a staggering number even in these circumstances, and came to various conclusions, some of them worth repeating here:[5]

- "The Board justifiably relied entirely on information provided by management. Under Delaware law, the directors are thereby immunized from personal liability."

- Valukas took much the same line with our management team: "The Examiner concludes that the conduct of Lehman's officers, while subject to question in retrospect, falls within the business judgement rule and does not give rise to colorable claims."

- He also did not find it necessary to accuse management of anything illegal: "The Examiner finds insufficient evidence to support a determination that Lehman's senior managers breached their fiduciary duty of candor, which required them to provide the Board with material reports concerning Lehman's risk and liquidity."

The Valukas Report has many references to the billions of dollars that were removed from Lehman's account by JPMorgan Chase in the days leading up to the fatal weekend.[6] Although the courts later upheld JPMorgan Chase's right to do so, the impact of their action surely goes a long way in explaining why the firm's liquidity diminished so rapidly.

· · ·

WHEN ONE TAKES A point of view that differs with conventional wisdom, it is truly comforting to find an objective person who agrees with you. I have long maintained that the decision to force Lehman Brothers into bankruptcy was the worst public policy decision of my lifetime. It froze the world's dollar flow and tipped global markets into five years of deep recession. It caused banks to stop lending or trusting in one another, which is fatal for the daily movement of trade and countertrade. And it could have been avoided. Dr. Laurence Ball is chairman of the Economics Department at Johns Hopkins University, and he agrees. In July 2016, he delivered a paper entitled "The Fed and Lehman Brothers" to the Monetary Economics Program of the National Bureau of Economic Research (NBER).[7] His paper is now a book, *The Fed and Lehman Brothers: Setting the Record Straight on a Financial Disaster*.

Dr. Ball spent several years after the September 2008 Lehman bankruptcy seeking answers to the question of why Lehman was the only large financial institution to file for bankruptcy. According to his research, this occurred when others "such as Bear Stearns and AIG, also experienced liquidity crises and surely *would* have gone bankrupt if not for emergency loans from the Federal Reserve." He goes on to ask, "Why didn't the Fed make another loan to rescue Lehman?"

Dr. Ball says that Ben Bernanke and others have stated that they "wanted to save Lehman, but could not do so because they lacked the legal authority." His paper tells of a speech Bernanke made in Jackson Hole, Wyoming, in 2009 in which Bernanke asserted the "company's available collateral fell well short of the amount needed to secure a Federal Reserve loan of sufficient size to meet its funding needs. As the Federal Reserve cannot make an unsecured loan . . . the firm's failure was, unfortunately, unavoidable."

Dr. Ball then goes on to state unequivocally that "the Fed did in fact have the authority to rescue Lehman," and concludes, "The available evidence supports the theories that political considerations were important, and that policymakers did not fully anticipate the damage from the bankruptcy. The record also shows that the decision to let Lehman fail was made primarily by Treasury Secretary Henry Paulson. Fed officials deferred to Paulson even though they had sole authority to make the decision under the Federal Reserve Act."

Dr. Ball wrote, as support for his conclusions, "There is a substantial record of policymakers' deliberations before the bankruptcy, and it contains no evidence that they examined the adequacy of Lehman's collateral, or that legal barriers deterred them from assisting the firm."

Further and most damning, Ball conducted a detailed examination of Lehman's finances and determined, "From a *de novo* examination of

Lehman's finances, it is clear that the firm had ample collateral for a loan
to meet its liquidity needs. Such a loan could have prevented a disorderly
bankruptcy, with negligable risk to the Fed. More specifically, Lehman
probably could have survived by borrowing from the Fed's Primary Dealer
Credit Facility [PDCF] on the terms offered to other investment banks.
Fed officials prevented this outcome by restricting Lehman's access to the
PDCF." This access to the PDCF was granted to the other investment
banks beginning on September 21.

Dr. Ball's book of more than 200 pages is well worth reading, since
he has done an exhaustive review of two fundamental sources that fully
chronicle the financial crisis of 2008 and the Lehman bankruptcy, those
being the aforementioned examiner report, prepared by Anton Valukas,
and the Financial Crisis Inquiry Commission, which was created by Congress. After reviewing thousands of pages, Ball stated that "the overall
record shows clearly that a Federal Reserve rescue of Lehman would have
been feasible and legal."

It is clear that federal actions saved AIG, Goldman Sachs, and could
have saved Lehman Brothers.

...

IMMEDIATELY AFTER THE BANKRUPTCY, in a decision that certainly val-
idated the talent on the Lehman board, the entire board, with the exception of Dick Fuld, was asked to stay on by Judge Peck, the bankruptcy
judge. As one of the younger members, I was chosen to be chairman of the
Lehman estate.

The crash was one thing. Cleaning up the mess was quite another. As
directors of the Lehman estate, we were to oversee what was left of Lehman
Brothers, and no one expected it to be anything but a long and difficult job.
Our task was onerous, and earning nothing more than a modest fee, we
developed a strategy never before practiced by a bankrupt company. Some
of my colleagues believed it could take fifteen years, but, in fact, Judge Peck

moved everything along at remarkable speed. To sell off Lehman's assets in the most profitable manner, we decided to take a five-year horizon. The strategy included selling some assets immediately and holding on to others until markets recovered. A third group had additional investments made by the Lehman estate, all with court approval. Our bankruptcy advisory firm, Alvarez and Marsal, did an amazing job of sorting out this gigantic financial mess. Because of their leadership, we were finished in about six years, at which point Lehman came out of bankruptcy.

After we had toiled away, salvaging what we could from the wreckage, a friend of mine, Tom Hill, head of hedge-fund investing at Blackstone, provided an interesting perspective during a round of golf we played. Tom told me that one of the best investments Blackstone had made in recent years was buying Lehman debt post-bankruptcy.

As it turned out, Lehman's assets proved to be worth much more than people were willing to recognize. Between late 2008 and February 2014, the value of the firm's assets more than tripled in value. The figures raise real doubts about the veracity of those people who had originally insisted that Lehman had an equity hole.

Today, Lehman is still managing and liquidating assets, with the proceeds going to the creditors.

Clearly, the Lehman bankruptcy presented the most difficult challenge in my lifetime. It is tough to pull "lessons learned" from this horrific experience. Surely, as I have stated, our board might have done some things differently to effect a different outcome. Management would, I am sure, say the same thing. And yet, no one broke laws, and no one could have predicted the confluence of major financial crises that occurred. It may simply be enough to say that when things seem too good, as financial markets were in the early 2000s, one best be a contrarian and seek cover—in other words, reduce risk.

Family

19

Suzanne and Family Life

T WAS AL TAUBMAN'S SIXTIETH birthday party at the River Club in New York in April 1985—an outrageous affair held in a needlessly tented ballroom awash with champagne. We watched, aghast, as waiters wheeled in huge baked potatoes onto which caviar was ladled, from champagne buckets, in great scoops.

But I shouldn't complain too much, because that evening I met Suzanne.

She was stunning in a sparkling, off-the-shoulder, dark green gown, and I quickly discovered that she and I were two of the few single people at the party. I was hoping we would be seated together, but that didn't happen. Suzanne found herself sitting next to Peter Duchin, the bandleader, while I was next to a new acquaintance named Amanda.

During cocktails, Suzanne came up and asked if anyone had ever told me I bore a resemblance to George H. W. Bush. Having recently moved from Washington, DC, I'd heard this comment more than once since my arrival. She then told me that he was her godfather and had given her away at her first wedding. Bush and her dad had been close friends ever since they were classmates at both Andover and Yale.

Suzanne Hooker being given away by her godfather,
George H. W. Bush, at her marriage to Ames Braga, January 1974.

**Republican
National
Committee**

George Bush, Chairman

January 15, 1974

Mrs. Ames Braga
250 East 73rd Street
New York, New York

Dear Suzanne:

It was great hearing from you. I am so glad you
sound so happy, and that all is going along okay up
there. Life has indeed been hectic. I am traveling
around the country all the time. Needless to say,
we'd love to see you if you get to Washington.

You asked about the Governorship in Texas. I
thought about running for Governor, but it seems
more important for me to stay in this job and try
to help build a strong Republican Party. I'll admit
it's not easy these days, but it is sure worthwhile
trying.

Give my love to your ma and thanks for your great
letter. One of the happiest days for me was the day
you and I walked down that aisle together. I was so
flattered and honored to have had you ask me to do
that.

We've got to see each other soon again. Best to Ames.

Love !!   Yours very truly,

                           George Bush

Dwight D. Eisenhower Republican Center: 310 First Street Southeast, Washington, D.C. 20003 (202) 484-6700

Letter of thanks from George H. W. Bush to Suzanne,
following her marriage to Ames Braga.

Michael Ainslie meeting George H. W. Bush in Washington, 1983.
Photo credit: Official Photograph, The White House.

We danced during the evening, and at intermission she asked if I played tennis. I said of course I did, and she asked if I would like to see the tennis courts in the lower levels of the River Club. She led me down a dark circular staircase to the courts, and I was impressed that she knew where the light switches were located. As we walked onto one of the two Har-Tru tennis courts, I noticed the board that listed the River Club champions, and I paused for a moment. I asked Suzanne to remind me of her last name. When she said Braga, I startled. There on the board was the name of the women's club champion for the past five years: Suzanne Braga.

"I don't play tennis," I immediately stated, reversing my earlier proclamation. However, I would make the mistake of going on the court to hit balls with her some months later when we started dating and honestly was worried she would end things between us right then and there. She was in a very different league.

On this night as the party broke up, I offered to give both Suzanne and Amanda a ride home. I dropped Amanda off first because she lived closer to the River Club, and Suzanne and I joked afterward that was the one reason I ended up marrying Suzanne.

It took awhile for our initial courtship to take off because I was a little slow on the draw. I was dating someone else at the time and trying to wind up the relationship, but I knew I had to put down a marker for this beautiful woman. Our plans for the summer did not coincide. Suzanne was going to be in Long Island's Southampton, playing tennis at the Meadow Club, while I was spending weekends in Tuxedo Park, where I had rented for the summer, near my dear friends Philip and Jayne Mengel. So I suggested that we have an understanding that we would get together in the fall in New York and get serious about our relationship. She found that more than a little odd, but it seemed to work, as we began seeing each other seriously when September came along.

The champion's board at the River Club reflected Suzanne's married name. She had been the wife of Ames Braga, whose father had been a Cuban sugar magnate before being ousted by Fidel Castro. When they were married, George H. W. Bush had in fact flown back from his post as envoy to China to give her away because her father, Edward Gordon Hooker, had passed away when she was twelve.

One of the challenges of our courtship was the difficult relationship both she and her sister, Peggy, had with their mother. It seemed Marian Hooker was quite jealous of her daughters, and she certainly didn't make things easy for us. To start with, I was obviously not her first or even second choice as a new husband for Suzanne. Since her divorce, Suzanne had been one of New York's most attractive and eligible young women and dated several guys with high profiles. In Mrs. Hooker's eyes, that put me way down the field.

But Suzanne and I were falling in love, and although the courtship took eighteen months, we began looking for an apartment together in the fall of 1986. When we applied to buy an apartment in the Upper East Side, Mrs. Hooker started interfering and told her good friend, who was the president of the building, that we would probably not be good tenants since we were bound to give noisy parties. My future mother-in-law also tried another tack; she told some of her friends that because I worked at Sotheby's, I had to be gay. Suzanne found that less than amusing. And since I had many gay friends and colleagues at Sotheby's and elsewhere, so did I.

It was not until Halloween of 1986 that I popped the question. I needed a couple of Jack Daniels at the 21 Club that night before I was able to pluck up the courage to tell Suzanne what I felt. "I would love for you to marry me," I said to her. Some months earlier, she had commented that anyone wanting to marry her had best propose properly on bended knee. She reminded me of this at that moment, and I quickly went down on one knee. We happened to be sitting at one of the banquettes just inside the entry to the club, so this necessitated pushing the table into the aisle to make room for my very public demonstration of my love for Suzanne. To my joy, I received a qualified yes. And as fate would have it, the man sitting two tables away from us was David Metcalfe, an English friend from London, so I even had a witness.

Suzanne and I flew to London in early November and stayed in our Sotheby's flat in Mayfair. We had been thinking of a February wedding, but after consuming the only items available in the flat—a tin of pâté and a bottle of champagne—we decided to get married in a few short weeks on December 13. Why wait with the prospective mother-in-law causing such a ruckus? So, returning to New York, we were soon married at the Church of the Heavenly Rest on Fifth Avenue at East Ninetieth Street by a tall, blond Englishman, the Reverend Hugh Hildesley, who ironically, in a different life, had worked at Sotheby's as an expert in old masters.[1]

The longer I was with Suzanne, the more I came to understand what an exceptional woman I had found. She was more than a partner, a lover, and a wife. She had become my best friend and my advisor on all aspects of my life. Better than any psychologist could have done, she talked me through the various problems that blew up during my volatile relationship with Al Taubman while I was at Sotheby's, and she was always there for me day and night.

Unfortunately, in those early years, I had to travel a great deal for Sotheby's, spending one week a month in London and traveling to Asia every two to three months. Although Suzanne came to London with me on occasion, the long-distance journeys were generally not for her, since she struggled with jet lag. We did take a stressful trip to Taiwan, Korea, and Japan at one point, during which Suzanne was held back in the Seoul airport because her passport didn't have a visa for our next destination in Taiwan. I was told to board the plane without her and, in spite of an important client waiting for me in Taipei, I wisely declined. We spent a crazy day running to embassies all over Seoul in order to get the necessary visa for Suzanne. We managed to catch a late-evening flight together, and I'm happy to say that the misadventure didn't end our marriage. My client was understanding, and my amazing wife was still my wife.

Suzanne mostly stayed in New York when I traveled. She had a full-time job in venture capital, working with Louis Marx at Wood River Capital, and kept herself busy with her own activities. This included playing tennis regularly at the River Club with Owen Williams and Gene Scott, both internationally ranked players in their day, and Peter Talbert, whose father, Billy, had been a Davis Cup captain and chairman of the US Open. Our dear friend Haigh Cundey was another regular in the evening doubles matches.

Suzanne has always been involved with health and fitness. Following this passion, in 1987, she started a new company called Gourmet Gazelle, a prepared food deli that operated from a small store at Seventieth Street and Third Avenue in New York City. Unfortunately, her company, with its low-sodium and low-fat menu items, was ahead of its time. It rang up lots of accolades but also an equal amount of losses before she folded it. She then started *Dining Smart, a Healthy Guide to Dining in New York*, and had some great fun being a restaurant critic. The guide was a popular success, but when we decided to move to Florida not long after our daughter was born, it was a casualty.

Suzanne and I moved around a lot in our first decade together, having lived in four different New York apartments, three different houses in Connecticut, and eventually four different homes in the Palm Beach area with our daughter. Everyone joked about our frequent change of address cards and how the National Association of Realtors should name us Family of the Year. We even made a spoof of this in one of our change of address cards one year.

At one point earlier on, we rented a place in Southampton for the summer, where Suzanne was heavily involved with tennis at the nearby Meadow Club. But Al and Judy Taubman had just restored a home on the beach there, and it became a bit miserable for us, with me having to deal with Al's demands for Sotheby's, and Suzanne with Judy's comments about the competitive nature of certain women at the Meadow Club. Neither Suzanne nor I were enjoying it, so we decided to escape to a more relaxing environment in subsequent years, instead renting a place at Lyford Cay in the Bahamas. During that time, I was able to catch a nonstop flight into Nassau from London, going straight there after business trips to Europe. Lyford Cay was a delightful spot for us, and we appreciated the summers we were able to spend together there.

It wasn't until I had left Sotheby's that Suzanne and I considered having a child. Her difficult relationship with her mother had initially left her lukewarm on the subject, but since I knew we were about to enter a new phase of life, I wanted to know if she felt any differently. Suzanne surprised me by saying she would love to have a child but on one important condition—that I stop traveling around the world like a madman. It was a reasonable request, given what my responsibilities had been over the years, and I was thrilled. When it became clear that we had accumulated an adequate net worth to live a comfortable life, we went ahead.

Although I was never formally offered the post, there was a brief discussion with my friend Nordeman around that time about the top job at the Museum of Modern Art being available if I was interested. It was more of a fundraising role, which did not interest me, particularly since I was already fully involved with Debbie Bial in building The Posse Foundation and doing lots of fundraising with her. I'd also promised Suzanne that I would not take on another demanding job, and I wanted to honor that promise to her. Though I was fifty-two years old; had a full portfolio of philanthropic, investment, and board service projects; and never considered myself retired, either then or now, I was very excited to become a full-time father again and wanted to make sure I was setting us up for the best situation possible.

...

WE WERE THRILLED WHEN Serena Hooker Ainslie arrived on January 16, 1998. Within ten days of her birth, we moved to Florida because we didn't want to bring up a child in New York and preferred a small town where we could all become involved in the community with lots of sports and good schools. Suzanne and I had looked around for the right place to move in the preceding months—Naples, Florida, and also Montecito, near Santa Barbara in California, which we loved. But we kept coming back to the advantages of the Palm Beach area with its weather and ease of transportation.

Moving to Palm Beach to live and to raise Serena was a wonderful move for our family. Our home was located two blocks from the Palm Beach Day Academy, the school she would attend. Most days Serena and I walked to school hand in hand. Her friends used our home as a hangout after school and on weekends, and we became close friends with many of their parents.[2] There was a great sense of community.

When Serena was ten years old, life took a dramatic turn for us after Lehman Brothers crashed in 2008. A healthy portion of our wealth was wiped out, and I was so fortunate that Suzanne became a willing and effective partner in a lifestyle adjustment. We had owned a comfortable apartment in Aspen, mostly for summer use, but after Lehman went down, we decided it was not essential. We sold the apartment, but more cuts were needed. Though we weren't left poverty-stricken, we recognized that our home in Palm Beach was an old and expensive house to run, and it turned out to be much smarter to sell it and build a beautiful new but smaller home in Palm Beach a little farther north. We also put a general cost-cutting program into effect on an everyday basis, which wasn't that difficult, because Suzanne has always been a person who has been more interested in the spiritual than the material.[3]

In middle school, Serena became a highly competitive tennis player, playing year-round and never having to be urged to go play or practice. She was also a great student, winning awards as the outstanding student in her school. And she was a focused, self-driven young lady. So it was not entirely a surprise when she told us in eighth grade that she wanted to look at boarding schools. "I want to get the best education I can get, and I don't think that is here in Florida!" she said. In 2012, she went to attend Deerfield Academy, a prestigious school in Massachusetts. She'd come close to picking the Hotchkiss School, a college preparatory school in Connecticut with a solid reputation, but after listening to her cousin Alexander Mejia speak about his own Deerfield experience with passionate expressions of love and affection, she chose Deerfield at the last minute.

Not surprisingly, Serena was a star at Deerfield. She was not only captain of the tennis and volleyball teams, but in addition she was selected to be head cheerleader, was a member of the Disciplinary Council, and graduated cum laude with top honors in history and Spanish.

Just a quick word about Serena's middle name, Hooker. It was, as I mentioned, Suzanne's maiden name, and over the years, both Suzanne and I have had fun telling new friends that I married a Hooker from New

York, just to see the shock on their faces.[4] But when it came time to name our daughter, we wanted to preserve not only Suzanne's name but also this interesting piece of family history. Serena had never been particularly thrilled with her middle name until later, when for a class project at Deerfield Academy, she was asked to research and explain the origins of her name and family. She learned that Suzanne and I had in fact always accurately explained the story: that her distant relative, General Joe Hooker, had been a Northern general in the Civil War and, being an attractive fellow, had lots of Southern belles following him and his men from campsite to campsite where they became known as Hooker's girls, or simply hookers. Upon learning the origins of this rather famous, or infamous, term, Serena came to appreciate the unique history behind her middle name. And she grew to be proud of it.

After Deerfield, she considered going on to Duke or Virginia, but she selected Vanderbilt, warming the heart of her father, who'd carefully kept his mouth shut during the selection process because he'd known that promoting Vanderbilt would almost certainly have led this strong-willed young woman to go elsewhere. Today, she is happily enrolled at Vanderbilt and hopes to graduate in May 2020.

Serena is a special young woman with an empathetic heart, a passion for justice, and a deep concern about the environment. She is nonjudgmental and has scores of friends. She makes her mother and me very proud.

...

SUZANNE AND SERENA ARE two of the people I love most dearly in this life. From them, I've learned so much about nutrition, spirituality, the environment, and how to relax and have fun.

20

The Riches of Family

I COULD NOT DISCUSS THE PEOPLE I love dearly in this world without mentioning all of my family, namely Katherine, Robbie, Liza, and Michael, and also my own siblings. They fill my heart, and I would not be who I am without them. Because of them, I know what it means to have the richness of a large and complex family and the love and support of them all.

I'm also deeply moved by the love and affection Suzanne developed for my four grown children and they for her. It was not always easy. When Suzanne and I married in 1986, Katherine was twenty-two, Robbie twenty-one, Liza nineteen, and my son, Michael, was only twelve.

Michael and Suzanne had an instant affinity. Both loved sports, particularly tennis, since Michael was then going to summer tennis camp at John Gardiner's in California. I can remember them throwing a football back and forth in Central Park on one of his regular visits to New York from DC where he lived with Lucy. We also took many wonderful skiing trips to Colorado and Austria during his years at the Westtown School, a Quaker boarding school he attended near Philadelphia.

For the girls, it was not so easy. I had a wonderful relationship with Lucy's three daughters. And they loved having a stepdad who took them to Europe for Sotheby's sales in Monte Carlo or to the races at Ascot near London. We often took spring break trips to the Caribbean and dined at the great restaurants of New York City. But adjusting to the arrival of a beautiful young woman in my life was understandably difficult for them. The two older ones had a hard time accepting Suzanne at first, and sadly, I had to tell them that Suzanne and I were extremely happy and that we very much wanted them in our lives but only when they were fully accepting of her in a loving way. It took a year or so of little contact, and they realized I was serious. To their great credit, they each began to build a strong, loving relationship with Suzanne, and that has only grown over the years.

All four of my older kids are today happily married with children of their own, pursuing their own paths and passions, and I could not be prouder of each of them.

...

KATHERINE, AFTER STUDYING AT Brown and NYU and a stint living in Maine, returned to her hometown of Savannah, Georgia, where her father—Tom Oxnard—and her grandmother Kay Scardino both live. She is a well-respected and published writer and community activist in Savannah. She married Blake Ellis, a wonderful, fun internet entrepreneur, and together, they are raising his two children, Jax and Drew.

I love telling the story of Katherine's comment upon learning that Jean Harris, the head mistress of Madeira, the school that Robbie and Katherine attended while we were in Washington, had just murdered her lover. "Don't worry, Dad, that school is bigger than any one woman." I thought this was impressive wisdom for a sixteen-year-old. Over the years, her words have also sometimes provided much-needed perspective to me and others during times of trial, reminding us that we can be bigger, transcending a difficult situation.

...

ROBBIE, AFTER STUDYING AT Barnard and then getting an MBA at Harvard, found the love of her life in David Bent, a talented architect who is a Duke graduate. They have restored a beautiful old coach barn in Riverdale, just north of New York.

Robbie played a vital role at The Posse Foundation where she served as executive director for several years while Posse Foundation founder Debbie Bial got her PhD at the Harvard School of Education. An incredibly strong and talented leader, she prepared Posse for its first expansion beyond New York City and then led the openings for Posse in Boston and Chicago. Today, Posse has built on that expansion model to operate in ten cities all over the country, and Robbie continues to play an important role on Posse's finance committee and as a board member.

Despite receiving an MBA from Harvard, she made a midlife decision to return to school for a second master's at Sarah Lawrence in English and is now a college teacher. She and David are raising two fabulous teenagers. Addison, a graduate of the Fieldston School in Riverdale and a talented chef and athlete, now attends Middlebury College. Their daughter, Clara, a promising artist, chose to go away to board at the Millbrook School and is thriving.

Robbie is a person who truly engages in introspection. She realized that while she was incredibly good at finance and management, it was not ultimately fulfilling for her. She knew that teaching and creative writing were fulfilling, so she went back to school and made a big change in her life. I am enormously proud of her for finding her passion.

...

LIZA HAS ALWAYS BEEN a singer-songwriter. After several years of singing and performing in Telluride, Colorado, she found Jesse Aratow, the love of her life and a fellow music professional. Jesse is an owner of

Madison House, a company that books musicians and markets and manages bands, including the String Cheese Incident, a well-known band with a near-cult following.

Liza and Jesse settled in Boulder, where Liza is a local legend and recognized for putting talent together for performances at the Fox Theater, a live music venue. She's traveled with her own bands, first ZUBA and now PIKZIL, and teaches guitar and singing to young aspiring musicians.

She's also a highly involved parent and Boulder activist. Their two children, Kalea and Lily, are a joy. Kalea is an athlete, like her mom, who was an all-state soccer player at her boarding school, Purnell, and then a water ski jumper at Rollins College, where her musical talent exploded. Kalea has spent years learning to become a gymnast, while Lily, much younger, just makes us laugh and hug her. Kalea celebrated her Bat Mitzvah in April 2019, following in the Jewish tradition of her father Jesse's family. The assembled family all smiled in joy as this young girl became a young woman.

Liza and her family remind me of the importance of finding joy every day in our lives. Liza does that, and it makes everyone around her better people.

...

LIFE IS FULL OF unexpected riches, and I believe that the relationship Suzanne and I have with my three stepdaughters and their families is one of the most valued of those. Since Suzanne and I are not the real grandparents of all the young brood I've described, we had to come up with names for our grandkids to call us. Suzanne had a famous aunt named Gigi who was married ten times, twice to the same lucky guy, and I've always been a rather active guy, so I liked the way Gogo sounded. We picked for ourselves Gigi and Gogo, two of the best names we could have dreamed of, and they stuck.

Suzanne and I feel incredibly blessed with close, loving relationships with all of these remarkable young women and their families. In June 2017, all nineteen of us in the extended Ainslie family gathered for a reunion at the well-named Reunion, Florida. It was a special time.

Ainslie family reunion, June 2017. From left to right: Robbie Bent, Michael Loren Ainslie, Michael Ainslie, Suzanne Ainslie with Dunckin, Liza Aratow, Katherine Ellis, and Serena Ainslie.

The Ainslie Family.

. . .

BEFORE MY DEAR SISTER, Ellen, passed away in May 2015, five years after she received a lung transplant, she'd told us that she wanted a party, not a funeral. We held Ellen's party, a celebration with more than sixty extended family and friends, at Robbie and Dave's beautiful home in Riverdale, gathering to remember our dear sister, cousin, aunt, and friend. It was a chilly evening in late September.

Suzanne, who loved Ellen and had been close to her, had asked, before my sister's passing, for Ellen to reappear in some form. Ellen told Suzanne that she would come back as a bird, in fact as a hummingbird. Miraculously, as we were getting ready for the party to begin, Suzanne and I walked out to the beautiful Bent garden overlooking the Hudson River, and there, in spite of the fact that hummingbirds hadn't been seen for weeks since fall had set in, was a hummingbird. Ellen, we knew, would not have missed her own party.

Also at Ellen's party were my brother David and his lovely wife, Rebecca. They live in Southern Pines, North Carolina, near Pinehurst where David is a community leader and Rebecca plays a leadership role in First Health, the regional hospital system. Their boys, Karl and Drew, live in nearby Asheville and Charlotte.

Our brother Peter passed away in 2008 but left two special Ainslies behind. Erin Ainslie, now Erin Ainslie Smith, a pediatric nurse, is the proud mother of Jagger and Stevie, whose names echo her father's love of music. Her brother Patrick married the charming Eunah Han, an up-and-coming clothing designer, in the summer of 2018. Patrick is one of the early employees of a high-tech company mapping the streets of our country for the upcoming era of autonomous vehicles.

. . .

MY SON MICHAEL'S EARLY years were a challenge for both Lucy and me, since he was only eight years old at the time she and I divorced. As I mentioned earlier, I shortly thereafter moved to New York to take on the Sotheby's job, and he stayed with Lucy in Washington. Though Michael and I saw each other on most weekends, he was understandably confused by the change in family dynamics and had a lot of anger. It took some years for us to truly become close again.

As a ninth grader, he headed off to the Westtown School, a boarding school in Pennsylvania, and I believe that neutral ground was conducive to our healing. After high school, he chose Hampshire College, a small liberal arts college in western Massachusetts, but after a year of playing around and not doing much studying, he came to me and said he was wasting his time and my money and would like to ski for a year or two. I told him that was fine but that he would have to support himself if that was his plan.

He, Suzanne, and I had a tearful departure from our home in Stamford, Connecticut, where I cut up his Visa card, gave him $500, and told him we would pay the insurance on his Jeep. He then departed for a new life adventure in Colorado with his girlfriend and his dog.

Little did I know that, realizing the difficult path he'd chosen for himself, he'd sought help by staying with my dear friends Jim and Dianne Light in Aspen, Colorado, as well as with others for the next several months. Looking back, Michael acknowledges that having to be independent and figure out how to survive during that time on his own was one of the best things that ever happened to him.

Over the next two years, he lived by his wits and by learning how to cook. It turned out that he really loved cooking and came back home awhile later saying that he wanted to become a chef and attend the New England Culinary Institute (NECI). He had done his research, and after a visit to the school, Suzanne and I agreed to help him. Off Michael went to a two-year culinary arts program at NECI. He interned at the Little Nell in Aspen under the great chef George Mahaffey and proved his talent and worth. Mahaffey told me on one visit, "Mike gets his work done so fast and with such passion, he reminds me of myself as a young chef."

Postgraduation, Michael moved full time to Aspen, joining Mahaffey at the Little Nell and eventually earning his place on the brigade that

Mahaffey led to win a James Beard award for Best Chef Southwest in 1997. After stints working with fine dining chefs in Seattle, New York, and San Francisco, he realized a new role was called for or he might suffer the fate of so many chefs who never get home until 1:00 AM each night and have little, if any, family life. Based on my McKinsey years, I encouraged him to seek culinary consulting firms and, within a year, he joined a small start-up consultancy in San Francisco. One of his clients, the UK based grocery chain Tesco, soon hired him to develop all the recipes for Fresh and Easy as part of its entry into the US grocery market. Along with his growing relationship with Kate Meyers, this precipitated his move to Los Angeles.

Michael loves to take on leadership roles in growth companies. He enjoyed a five-year stint at Pitfire Pizza, running operations while building and opening seven new restaurants. Border Grill became his first CEO position, where he repositioned its restaurants in LA and Las Vegas. This was a great learning experience, as it was a challenging brand with strong and diverse owners. We talked often, and I encouraged him to keep up his lifelong habit of writing down the good and the bad management techniques that he learned from owners and bosses.

Tired of challenging bosses, Michael set up his own consulting firm, which enabled him to take a more active role in helping Kate raise their two children. His passion for the design/build process for new restaurants has led him to a great new consulting assignment as Owner's Representative for a large new restaurant in the Chase Center in San Francisco, the new arena and home of the Golden State Warriors. This did not disappoint their son Noah, as Klay Thompson and the entire Warriors team are his heroes.

Michael looks ahead to a senior management role in the culinary world, and I am excited to see where his skills and experiences can lead.

Kate Meyers was a third grade classmate from the Beauvoir School in DC. She remembered Michael fondly and, after his divorce, was excited to be reintroduced to him by Simon Lamb, Michael's half brother. After a romantic camping trip involving lobster and Cristal, she was swept off her feet, and their romance ensued. Having gotten her doctorate in psychology, Kate was busy building a successful counseling practice and before long, they were engaged. Michael moved to LA to join Kate in the charming bungalow she had purchased in Culver City.

July 28, 2007, saw them joined in a spectacular wedding at the beachfront home of Kate's mother in Rye, New Hampshire. The best toast of the wedding came from Mrs. Fotheringill, their third-grade teacher from the Beauvoir School, who had somehow been rediscovered by Kate's dad. Mrs. Fotheringill had us all in stitches during her toast as she read from Michael's and Kate's third-grade papers. Kate, a six-foot-tall gorgeous redhead, had stated in her paper that her life goal was to be a gymnast. And Michael, also very tall at six feet, five inches, had said in his paper that his dream was to be a jockey.

Michael and Kate live happily in Culver City, California, raising two of the most special kids, ten-year-old Noah Hopper and seven-year-old Emmaline Faith Carpenter Ainslie. Noah is a huge Warriors fan, so his dad's new job makes him very happy.

From a dad's perspective, I treasure the loving, supportive relationship Michael and I have developed; he comes for advice when he needs it. Suzanne and I adore his family and the values he and Kate are instilling in their children. And we admire that Michael and Kate are both successful, independent, highly focused professionals and parents doing what they love.

What more could a father want?

. . .

TO ME, AMONG THE greatest of investments you can ever make in your life is your family. I am most proud that my children have pursued their passion, even when it was not the most obvious or lucrative profession; they are doing what they love, and as a result, they are great parents and happy spouses.

Changing the Trajectory of Vanderbilt

21

A University That Makes Opportunities Happen

MY ALMA MATER, VANDERBILT UNIVERSITY, has risen to become one of America's highest-rated universities, and I was grateful to have the opportunity to help steer that growth during my twenty-one years on its board of trustees. I have always felt that Vanderbilt truly launched me on the wonderful life I have enjoyed, so I've always been compelled to generously give back.

During my tenure, the board made several big decisions that have changed the trajectory of Vanderbilt University. The first came long ago in 1989 when Vanderbilt became the first university to welcome The Posse Foundation, an amazing educational nonprofit, and Posse's annual group of ten scholars to its undergraduate program. The university not only paved the way for these young scholars but also gave Posse the credibility to build a university partner network that today includes nearly sixty leading universities.

It was a huge thrill to welcome a Posse scholar, Dr. Shirley M. Collado, now the president of Ithaca College, to the Vanderbilt board as my term ended. Shirley was in that first Posse group at Vanderbilt in 1989 and went on to get her PhD at Duke, become vice president and dean of the College at Middlebury, and take on the position of provost at Rutgers University-Newark; now she is a university president. She demonstrated the value of and need for the Posse program and exemplified the qualities of a scholar and leader. Posse graduates becoming board members and leaders of organizations have always been some of Posse's long-term goals, and I'm thrilled that Vanderbilt made a high-quality and academically rigorous education a reality for Shirley and so many others.

In more recent years, Vanderbilt has continued to show its appreciation for the quality of Posse graduates by appointing a second Posse alumnus to the board. Kito Huggins had demonstrated leadership skills even as an undergraduate student at Vandy in the early 1990s by serving as the president of the Student Government Association. He went on to attend Vanderbilt University Law School, earning his degree in 1999, and is today the director of executive administration at a major Manhattan law firm.

During the past few decades, no one has had a greater impact on Vanderbilt than Nicholas S. Zeppos, the chancellor from 2008 to 2019. Previously a law professor and the university provost, Nick is a fun and gregarious human being, a great public speaker, and a remarkable leader. Nick recently completed his eleven-year stint as chancellor, but I will always view him as my chancellor.

Nick led the Vanderbilt Board of Trust through a long consideration of creating a residential college system, much like those at Ivy League schools or Oxford and Cambridge in the United Kingdom. First would come the freshman commons, opening in 2008 as The Martha Rivers Ingram Commons, in recognition of former Board of Trust Chairman Martha Ingram's board and philanthropic leadership, which helped create a remarkable living and learning experience at Vanderbilt. The Ingram Commons, comprising 10 "houses" arranged around a quadrangle where all first-year students and also many faculty members and their families live, became a pivotal focal point of change at Vanderbilt. Among other things, students found themselves living in a dynamic, multigenerational atmosphere where the experience of interacting with fellow students, world-class faculty, parents, children, and even dogs helped them to grow as people.

This project was a bold step for Vanderbilt that saw the board unify behind a big initiative to build the university into something even greater. Subsequently, other residential colleges for sophomores, juniors, and seniors have been and continue to be constructed, with plans for four new ones underway at a cost of $600 million. Nick has been instrumental in transforming residential life at Vanderbilt for the better and improving the quality and breadth of the student experience.

Of course, these accomplishments could not have been achieved without the generosity of Martha Ingram and her family, as Mrs. Ingram and the Ingram Charitable Fund have made many high-impact contributions to Vanderbilt over the years. When Bronson Ingram died tragically of brain cancer in 1995, his wife, Martha, who had before been mainly involved in Ingram's charitable activities, took over leadership of the company and became a successful CEO, leading Ingram Industries for more than thirteen years. She also chaired the Vanderbilt board from 1999 until 2011, and I was honored to work with her. In her philanthropic life, she has not only helped make Vanderbilt a better, stronger university but also led in the creation of world-class performing arts centers in Nashville and in her hometown of Charleston, South Carolina.

John Ingram, who built Ingram Book Company into what is today Ingram Content Group, fortunately followed his mother onto the Vanderbilt board and has been extremely involved in the athletics program. In one of my last roles as a board member, John and I worked together with Vice Chancellor Nick Zeppos and Athletics Director David Williams, and others on the search committee to recruit and hire James Franklin, an outstanding football coach whom we managed to pry away from the University of Maryland. Coach Franklin is an amazing leader who transformed the Vanderbilt football program, taking us to bowl games in each of his three years at the university. Some of his players have gone on to play at the highest levels of the NFL, and he has since moved on to Penn State to become its head coach. A few years after he left, he and I had the opportunity to sit together at a Vandy baseball game when he was back in Nashville for the wedding of one of his Vandy players. In a wonderful moment, he expressed his appreciation for the opportunity we gave him at the university. For me, it was a reminder once again of the high caliber of talent and amazing quality of experience that the board at Vanderbilt was able to help bring about.

Nick also led another big policy change at Vanderbilt. Some years ago, he began suggesting to the board of trustees that the university adopt a "no loan" approach to financial aid so that students would no longer need to take out any need-based loans to receive an education, a program we called Opportunity Vanderbilt. Remarkably, the program launched in 2008, right in the midst of the post–Lehman Brothers financial meltdown, which hit Vanderbilt as hard as it did every other institution in the world. Nonetheless, Nick persevered, and the program has been a triumphant success—in its first 11 years, more than $400 million has been raised in new endowment and current-use gifts, enabling all student aid to be in the form of grants and work study.

As a result, the number of entrance applications has soared at Vanderbilt, from around 17,000 in 2008 to more than 37,000 in 2019, arriving from bright kids who could have not previously afforded a Vandy education and who did not want to take on a mountain of debt. While Nick and the board had to go out and raise a lot of money to make this happen, the significant increase in both the quantity and quality of applicants showed how welcomed it was to families on a tight budget. The competitive set of universities our applicants are considering are now Duke, Harvard, Princeton, and Yale. Twenty years ago, they were Duke, Emory, Washington University, and the University of Virginia. This may seem a subtle change, but it's an important and noteworthy one. We're proud of our efforts to make this an opportunity for students.

Led by Nick, these big policy changes, which were shaped with heavy board involvement, have transformed Vanderbilt. Few universities have anything comparable to the Ingram Commons and the overall residential college experience at Vanderbilt, and only a handful have a "no loan" financial aid program.

The final major policy decision during my tenure on the board was again led by Chancellor Zeppos, aided by the brilliant strategist from Harvard Business School, Michael Porter. Vanderbilt University and Vanderbilt University Medical Center had always been combined in one corporate entity, exposing each to the risks and challenges of the other. Vanderbilt's medical center, a $4 billion clinical and research enterprise, sees more than 2.4 million patients a year, and Vanderbilt's School of Medicine ranks among the top twenty nationwide.

In recent years, virtually all other academic medical centers have been separated from the parent university to create separate governance and financial structures. The reasons are many but include the very different risk profiles of the two different businesses, the high leverage taken on by most hospitals and medical centers, and the significant uncertainty of payment schemes dealt with by hospitals. By contrast, universities are much more predictable and slower to change.

Michael Porter led our board in looking at the examples set by four other universities—Harvard, Duke, Northwestern, and Washington University—that had successfully managed this separation to determine how best to move forward. We knew it was a delicate operation, guided by the need to make sure one or both of the institutions wouldn't be damaged in the process. Nick then led the board through case studies of the four universities we studied, presenting strategic advice from Porter and recommending a plan for separation. The board approved the plan, which was implemented in the spring of 2016. As part of this, the board and other leaders at Vanderbilt learned from the experience and used it to develop a best-in-class approach. Both institutions are thriving following the separation.

Clearly, this was another example of Nick's remarkable leadership. Although I was an active board participant in each of these decisions, I claim no major responsibility for these important and critical policy decisions. They were driven by Nick Zeppos, someone I admire and have learned a great deal from. Nick is one of the great CEOs I have worked with, demonstrating an acute understanding of the big issues facing higher education. Under his leadership, Vanderbilt's board of trust worked to fundamentally redirect a well-established institution, which was no easy task but one that was critical for its future growth and health. In Nick's time, the endowment increased from a low of $2.9 billion after the financial crisis of 2008 to $6.4 billion, including, outside of investment returns, $2.6 billion in new monies added to the endowment during his tenure.

Today, Vanderbilt University ranks in the top fifteen of all American research universities, which is a number well above its standing some twenty years ago. This is largely the legacy of Nick Zeppos.

Throughout these years, Vanderbilt University has grown, helping to transform the vibrant city of Nashville along with it. The university and its medical center employ more than 33,000 people, making Vanderbilt the largest private employer in Nashville and the second-largest private employer based in Tennessee, which ensures that the university plays a central role in the well-being of the city and the state. Being able to participate in Vanderbilt University's growth as a board member has given me great satisfaction over the years, especially given the pivotal role it played in my early life.

It was a great privilege to serve on the Vanderbilt Board of Trust for twenty-one years, ending in June 2014 with my retirement to emeritus status. In my time on the board, I learned that strong academic institutions can evolve and change. All it takes is inspiring, committed leaders and a strong and generous board and alumni group.

Finding My Posse

22

The Posse Foundation

N 1989, FIVE SEVENTEEN-YEAR-OLD KIDS—FOUR girls and a guy— boarded a Greyhound bus with their mothers in New York City and set off on a twenty-six-hour ride to Nashville, Tennessee. The kids who got on the bus did not have a lot of money, were not necessarily the most academically accomplished students from their various public schools, and hadn't made top SAT scores. But they'd been invited to join in a pioneering experiment and participate in an innovative new program. The students had each been specially selected because of their drive, intelligence, vision, and ability to communicate. They'd been chosen because they had, even in their high school years, already demonstrated themselves to be leaders. They were headed for Vanderbilt University under a new program called Posse, and that bus ride was only the beginning of their journey.

The name Posse was what the whole thing was all about. Its idea came from a young woman named Debbie Bial—a graduate of Brandeis University—who was working with the City Kids Foundation in New York when she held a focus group for kids who had gone to college but dropped out. She wanted to better understand the factors that had led to their dropout. She remembers that one young man in the group, mumbling and a little flustered, had said, "I would never have dropped out of college if I had had my posse with me." That struck a chord and changed something in Debbie.

Debbie Bial is someone who listens well, and, as she recounts, at that moment, a light went on in her head. She understood that the young man had been saying that he'd felt alone, that he'd missed the support of his friends, kids he'd grown up with and gone to high school with who'd always been there for him. She realized that he'd needed them, and they needed him. He and his friends had been loyal to one another, a constant source of support in times of challenge, but he'd lost that once he started college. He'd lost his "posse." She wondered if it would be possible to send a group of students to college together where they could support one another. Posse was born then and there.

The opportunity to become involved with Posse arrived at a time in my life when I was trying to find a new passion after leaving Sotheby's. I was fifty-two years and still had a great deal of drive and energy. I wanted to do something meaningful but something outside the world of art. Though I'd enjoyed so many aspects of turning around Sotheby's, by the end of my time there, I was offended by the sometimes ostentatious nature of art collecting. In that time, collecting seemed to have become all about money. Buyers from Russia, collectors from Japan, and even individuals like Australian entrepreneur Alan Bond were splashing out huge sums of money, simply to massage their egos and heighten their profiles. It seemed less about the art and more about an easy way for rich people to become visible overnight; someone could buy a Monet, Renoir, or Picasso, and the public would suddenly want to know who that person was. I was put off by that and had gotten weary of this aspect of the art-collecting subculture. Of course, many of the clients I'd worked with were serious art collectors and had a deep love for and understanding of great works of art, but they were unfortunately getting elbowed aside and literally outbid by investment bankers and newly minted centimillionaires who simply wanted to be well known on the world stage. I hoped to put my efforts into a field that might make more of a difference in the lives of people who didn't have all those advantages.

I did some soul searching and started looking for a way to make a positive, lasting impact in people's lives, and as I did this, my mind kept coming back to the field of education. At the time, I was already involved with Vanderbilt University as a trustee when Susan Alexander, head of Human Resources at Sotheby's, told me of hearing about Posse at a cocktail party in New York. After I discovered Posse, I realized it offered a remarkable chance to do something important—something that would be valuable for thousands of talented young people. I also knew that a program like this would add incredible value to the country itself. In creating the opportunity for students with great potential to receive a world-class education, we could help build up leaders who might later become CEOs, board members, senators, or university presidents—leaders who would represent the true diversity of our country.

Posse appealed to me for many reasons. I myself had started out in life with a wonderful family and upbringing but little else. We had not been a family of great financial means, and my parents had not been able to afford a college education for me and my siblings. My life has been blessed because of many people and scholarship opportunities that enabled me to go on to receive a good education. But I could see that so many kids did not have these opportunities or avenues. They attended bad high schools, came from tough neighborhoods, and were not offered access to great universities.

The more young people I met through Posse, the more I came to realize how much untapped talent they possessed yet how limited their opportunities were. Without The Posse Foundation, they would likely not be able to change the trajectory of their lives. I felt I could help do something about this and decided to direct my energies toward building up this organization, and these students, for success.

I'd developed a wonderful friendship with Debbie, a woman of enormous ability. When I first met her, I could see that she was a smart and charismatic leader. The chance to partner with her in building Posse was irresistible. I learned from Debbie that the first couple of Posses had already been sent to Vanderbilt University but that as a result Posse was carrying a sizeable debt of $500,000 owed to Vanderbilt. Posse had taken on the responsibility to pay for the scholarships but was having trouble raising the money. The idea that a bunch of inner-city kids with generally low test results could succeed at a leading university was an audacious one. I loved a challenge, but I loved even more what I felt this organization could do.

At the same time that Posse's mission and heart intrigued me, my interest was tweaked even further by the fact that the kids had gone to Vanderbilt, my alma mater. There seemed to be a perfect alignment between my passion for education, my love for Vanderbilt, my desire to create opportunities for kids, and my professional experience. I believed, as I had done with other companies, that I could help make Posse a stronger, better organization.

...

WHEN THE FIRST POSSE arrived at Vanderbilt, they were greeted with a certain level of skepticism in the conservative southern city of Nashville. There was a slightly sarcastic tone in the local newspaper headlines after they arrived: "New York Posse Hits Nashville"—that sort of thing. Terry Deal was the professor who had persuaded Vanderbilt to go with the experiment, and he quickly gained the support of Bob Innes and many of the faculty at Vanderbilt. Some may have been a bit dubious when they examined the SAT scores of one of the first Posse students, Shirley Collado, whose scores were in the low 900s, combined.

Shirley's dad, a New York cab driver, was upset at the thought of his daughter going so far away to college. But Shirley's mother, a factory worker, and Shirley's maternal grandmother didn't want her to pass up the opportunity and, encouraged by Debbie Bial, helped organize the mothers of other Posse students as they prepared for the trip south.

As it turned out, no one needed to have worried. Not only did all five students in the first Posse graduate within four years, but also many of them did so with honors; Shirley, in particular, embraced the experience and became a star. She started the Association of Hispanic Students; joined the Original Cast, a performing arts organization; led students on two spring break trips to South America; and excelled at the Peabody School of Education at Vanderbilt, graduating as one of its most distinguished scholars. Her accomplishments earned her a full scholarship to Duke University for its PhD program in psychology. She was one of only seven students nationally to be selected for this program. And when Shirley earned her doctorate a few years later, she became the first Posse graduate to have done so.

Dr. Shirley Collado's progress since then has been nothing short of meteoric. She became vice president of student affairs and dean of the college at Middlebury, then executive vice chancellor and chief operating officer of Rutgers University in Newark, New Jersey. In the summer of 2017, Shirley became the president of Ithaca College. What a moment for this amazing young woman, the first-ever Dominican American president of a four-year college or university in the US.

When I eventually retired from the Vanderbilt Board of Trust in 2014, Shirley joined the board in the class that replaced me. One year later, she was selected secretary of the board and is today one of the most respected members of the Vanderbilt Board of Trust. In fact, she now sits on the search committee that will select the next chancellor of Vanderbilt University.

The success of Shirley and her fellow Posse members obviously allayed many of the fears people had. Suddenly, there was proof that kids who didn't test well could not only do university-level work academically but also become leaders on campus, succeeding in areas no one would have predicted. They performed at a high caliber and contributed in important ways to university life, enriching the experiences of students and faculty alike. Thanks to the first group of Posses who had paved the way, other outstanding young students, many from difficult backgrounds, would be invited to elite universities like Vanderbilt.

Debbie Bial emphasizes the fact that Posse is a strength-based initiative rather than a need-based program that gives a helping hand to under-privileged kids. It offers a leadership diversity program to top universities, sending the universities kids who, as Debbie puts it, "have the same dreams and abilities as privileged kids and are as meritorious as anyone else."[1] She believes that too often black advancement in America is seen as something offered to an underclass by rich white people. But "Posse kids don't need any favors other than a door that is not closed, an opportunity that they can be accepted on merit," she says. For that reason, Posse has and always will be a merit-based leadership scholarship program.

Vanderbilt and the other universities that became Posse partner universities soon discovered they had in their midst a group of exceptional young people who went about creating their own success through the use of their own skills and ambitions. They had simply earned the right to be there on the basis of a different evaluation of their talents. And they in fact became leaders on campus. The numbers show that, across different campuses, 80% of the 2017 Posse scholar graduates served as officer of some campus organization.[2]

Becoming a Posse scholar is not easy. Once nominated by a teacher, a coach, a rabbi, or a community leader, the Posse applicants go through three rounds of selection in what is known as the Dynamic Assessment Process. In these eight hours, Posse staff get to know the applicants, their strengths, their ambitions, and the ordeals they have endured. They ensure they have a holistic view of the candidates rather than a simplistic one based on only SAT or ACT scores or high grades. In 2018, The Posse Foundation received 15,000 nominations for kids, but only 770 made it.

The application program is rigorous, and once selected, the scholars begin an eight-month training program, which includes weekly three-hour sessions with their Posse at the local Posse office. It is in this Pre-Collegiate Training program that the Posse is shaped and the tight bonds are formed that will carry the students to success at college. A Posse typically has ten kids of different ethnic backgrounds—including Caucasian, Hispanic, Asian, and African American.

Posse scholars possess a four-year graduation rate of 90%, a metric that astonishes all the experts. But Debbie believes that finding exceptional people who have the attributes to make their own way in life is what Posse is all about.

...

THE HIGH STANDARDS DEBBIE established were part of the reason I wanted to help her. And when we first met, she did need help. She was young and, up to that point, had not had much fundraising experience. She operated on a shoestring budget from a borrowed office on Wall Street and struggled to pay her small staff.

In those early days, Posse was trying to raise the dollars to pay the cost of scholarships. This approach was clearly going to limit growth, since the dollars quickly got quite large. I suggested to Debbie that we try a different approach. "Why not let the university put up the scholarship money, since we're bringing them outstanding young people who will have a very positive impact on campus life," I told her. "These are students whom they can't really find on their own." Debbie was game to try this approach. So in 1994, we formed The Posse Foundation as a nonprofit foundation or, as some call it, a 501(c)(3), and I agreed to serve as chairman. Debbie became executive director, and we began to build a board. Building the board was great fun. First, we wanted passion for the program, and second, we wanted financial resources.

But I had some selling to do because we had to get the financial structure for Posse fixed. My first call was to Joe Wyatt, then the chancellor at Vanderbilt, because I knew what a highly favorable impression the first Posses had already made on him. I also had, at that time, recently been invited to become a Vanderbilt trustee and felt I was in a good position to go to Joe with an audacious proposal because the university had its eye on me as a future donor. "I know you have the scholarship money in your financial aid budget," I told him. "So if you pay for the scholarships, we'll find you the kids." Then I went even further, saying, "Since we'd effectively be part of your admissions department, helping you find these young stars, we'd like you to pay The Posse Foundation an annual fee of $25,000. And, by the way, when we work all this out, we'll pay you the $500,000 that Posse owes you."

After a few days of consideration, Joe—bless him—called to tell us he agreed, although he did ask us to waive the $25,000 annual fee for three years. We did waive it then, but it later became a fixture in Posse's revenue stream. Today, all fifty-seven university partners pay a $35,000 annual fee for each Posse they accept. This produces more than $2.6 million in recurring revenue to The Posse Foundation, since there are now seventy-seven Posses selected each year. (Seventy-seven Posses from fifty-seven universities because many of our university partners take a posse from more than one city; the University of Wisconsin, for example, takes Posses from four cities.) And Joe Wyatt went on to become a real Posse advocate. When speaking at our first fundraising luncheon, ironically held at Christie's New York galleries, Joe proclaimed, "Posse is not a program; it is a movement."

With Chancellor Wyatt's agreement to change the funding model, I went to work raising the cash. The Ainslie Foundation, our family foundation, put up half the money, and I went to see my friend Gene Shanks, a fellow Vandy trustee and then president of Bankers Trust, about providing the rest. Bankers Trust agreed. Gene then agreed to join the Posse board, where he has worked and served by my side for the past twenty years. After several years of hard work, The Posse Foundation was on its feet financially.

However, there were rough waters ahead. After Rice and Lehigh, a top engineering school in Pennsylvania, joined the program, we seemed to be going along quite well, but then a conflict arose that caused Rice and Lehigh to drop out. It happened because a jealous educator convinced them that her nonprofit could create an even better program. She was sadly unable to do so, however, and Lehigh rejoined Posse some years later. This loss was a near-fatal blow at the time, but leaning heavily on Vanderbilt's prestige as one of the nation's most respected universities, we got Posse back on track after a while.

...

AS I MENTIONED, TODAY, thanks to the fifty-seven universities that partner with The Posse Foundation, we select and place seventy-seven different Posses annually, and that number will continue to grow.[3] We recruit Posses from ten cities throughout the country. Since 1989, more than 9,200 kids have reaped the benefits of higher education at some of America's finest universities through The Posse Foundation. They have received more than $1.4 billion in scholarships. And, to restate, 90% of them are graduating.

The vision, dedication, and leadership Debbie Bial brings to Posse and its scholars are extraordinary. She has grown enormously over the thirty-year history of Posse. I have never seen a founder grow like Debbie. Today, she has personal relationships with scores of university presidents, oversees 165 staff members in ten Posse sites all over the country, and succeeds in raising Posse's $25 million annual operating budget, never having run a deficit. And for good measure, she has raised an $85 million endowment through operating surpluses and an incredible amount of generosity from many of our board members. In the process, she was named a recipient of the MacArthur "Genius" award and has seen Posse chosen by President Obama as one of ten charities to which he gave money from his Nobel Peace Prize.

In 2007, feeling new leadership could take Posse to another level, I stepped down as chairman of the board of The Posse Foundation after thirteen years. After a deliberative process, Jeff Ubben, one of our younger board members, was selected as my successor. Jeff's father, Tim Ubben, had been one of our early board stalwarts. As chairman of the board of DePauw University and a leading figure in Chicago, Tim brought to Posse many new university partners, board members, donors, and, fortunately, his son Jeff. Jeff had attended Duke and Northwestern's Kellogg School and founded Value Act, a successful private equity firm in San Francisco. Tim and Jeff Ubben have been Posse's most generous supporters. At the time of Posse's twenty-fifth anniversary in 2014, they each contributed $25 million to Posse. This formed the core of what has now become the $85 million endowment.

Michael Ainslie and his Posse scholar friends at
his retirement as Posse board chair, October 17, 2007.

About half of our thirty-five board members have significant wealth, but all the board members, regardless of their financial means, are incredibly great people who are passionate about Posse. They all bring total commitment to the table and exude Posse love. We have become our own little community, brothers and sisters committed to a cause, engendering a deep affection for the kids. We personally invest our time and care into the students, helping many of them find summer jobs and getting to know them.

Jamaal Nelson is a former Posse scholar and one who inspires me. His story, concerning an unpleasant incident during his time at Vanderbilt, demonstrates how forgiveness can overcome evil and enhance two lives instead of wrecking one. In 1995, when Jamaal was running for student body president at Vanderbilt, he discovered the picture of a noose scrawled on a flyer that advertised a campus-wide speech being given by Colin Powell. The flyer read, "Can a Black Man Be President?" but the words "Black" and "Man" had been crossed out, and Jamaal's name, as well as a noosed figure, had been drawn in. This ugly flyer had been taped to Jamaal's dorm room door, and the heinous act brought home a horrible realization that maybe Vanderbilt was not ready for racial change, not ready to see a talented young black orator become a student leader, not ready to see this New York kid who had arrived only three years earlier, severely dyslexic, move further in his career.

Jamaal's Posse convinced him to confront his fellow students and make this a teaching moment. The alternative, which Jamaal seriously considered, was to drop out of the race for Student Government Association (SGA) president, to let the pain take over, and to maybe even quit school.

Instead, on the following night, he spoke up, addressing a group of some 200 students at a "Snapple Chat" meeting in his residence hall.

"Can any of you conceive of the horrible memories a noose conjures up for a young black man?" he cried out. "Do you realize that, only decades ago, midnight hanging of black men was not uncommon, and not far from us here in Nashville?"[4] Jamaal, with his Posse squarely behind him, decided he was not ready to quit. "Is the person who painted this noose on my poster here in this room?" he asked. A long pause ensued, with a lot of people staring at the floor. Minutes went by with nothing being said until finally, a lanky white student in the back spoke up.

"I did it, and I feel horrible. I want to apologize. I did not understand the history of lynching and its horrific impact, still today, on young black men."

What happened next is still emblazoned on the memory of every student there that night. Jamaal walked up to the young man, embraced him with a huge hug, and uttered the three most beautiful words in the English language: "I forgive you." Jamaal went on to win the presidency of the Vanderbilt SGA, becoming only the third African American to do so in Vanderbilt's long 130-year history.

Less than a year later, I sat in a board of trust meeting in which Jamaal spoke eloquently, pleading with the board to raise funds to create an expanded center for student activities, a place for organizations to work and meet, for events to occur that would enliven the student experience for all. My friend and fellow trustee, Gene Vaughn, was so moved that he pledged $1 million on the spot, and soon the necessary $10 million was raised. The building stands today, a lasting reminder and tribute to that remarkable night when Jamaal demonstrated courage in the face of adversity, allowing many young people to learn a powerful lesson.

During the spring of Jamaal's senior year, I received a phone call from him. His incredibly deep, sonorous voice was unmistakable. "Mr. Ainslie," he said, "I have some great news. I have been given a full ride for theology school at Yale!" I shouted my congratulations, but he had more good news. "I also have an offer of a full scholarship to Harvard Divinity School. Where do you think I should go?" I believe that since he knew I had gone to Harvard Business School, he expected me to lean in that direction. Instead, I put it back to him.

"Jamaal," I said, "I think you know which one is right for you."

His reply was swift. "Yes, I think I will just have to go to HAAR-VAARD!" I was thrilled, not for Harvard but for Jamaal.

Jamaal is a true outlier. He had low SAT scores, totaling a combined 900, which would never have gotten him into Vanderbilt, but his natural leadership and public speaking skills were remarkable. Debbie Bial and Posse saw this and convinced Vanderbilt to take a chance. In his first days there, the Vanderbilt Learning Center discovered that Jamaal was severely dyslexic and could not read. He quickly learned to do so. He worked incredibly hard, graduated with a 3.6 GPA, and almost won a Rhodes scholarship. He is living proof of the fact that SATs are a horrible predictor of success in college or in life.

Today, Jamaal is an ordained minister, having started his own church in Harlem. He is married with three children. And he served as an elected district leader in Harlem and has recently taken on a leadership role in the education reform movement, working tirelessly to improve public education for young people in his community. There was a moment in Jamaal's life when the image of a noose had troubled him, threatening his sense of hope. But with the support of his Posse, he proved strong enough to cut it down, face its vile significance head-on, and do God's work.

It is hard to properly express the joy it has given me to witness the success of people like Jamaal Nelson, Shirley Collado, Kito Huggins, and so many others. Many have been winners of the Ainslie Alumni Achievement Award, an award given to one exceptional Posse alumnus each year. This award was created in 2008 upon my retirement as Posse board chairman, and as of the date of this writing, ten exceptional young leaders have now won it. They are out there in the world, building charter schools, creating water filtration companies in Kenya, teaching at universities like Yale Medical School, and doing truly exceptional things. Nothing makes me prouder than to be able to join them each August at the Posse Alumni Day to welcome the new Ainslie award winner.

...

ALL OF THIS CAME about due to the amazing work of Debbie Bial and her team and their excellent partnership with Posse's board and our incredible university partners. As a result, thousands of young people have been given the opportunity to go to college and make the most of their natural talents. Almost all of the students have grabbed that chance and made the most of what Posse offered them.

I have often wondered how things would have turned out for me had I decided to take another full-time job in my early fifties. I am so glad I didn't. Having been able to have a beneficial effect on the growth of Posse is enormously heartwarming for me, but it also turned out to be the right decision for my own family. I honored the commitment I made to Suzanne when we decided to have a child, making myself available to invest so much more heavily in Serena's life and upbringing. Had I been working full time, I would not have been able to be nearly as engaged with Posse, where the kids became like a second family to me.

Recently, when I was heading up to visit a doctor in New York, I called up Carlos Carela, a winner of the Ainslie award who is now an entrepreneur in the Bronx, involved in the wine business, and dealing in Cuban, Haitian, and Dominican Republic art. I looked forward to meeting my old friend Carlos but did not expect him to offer to stay with me for eight hours while I went through various tests at the hospital. It was a wonderful, loving gesture, and I was greatly touched by it. But then again, Carlos is a Posse guy. He had my back.

. . .

POSSE CELEBRATED ITS 30TH anniversary with a fabulous gala at the Metropolitan Museum's Temple of Dendur in May 2019. The gala brought more than 700 Posse supporters and scholars and raised more than $3.2 million.

Michael Ainslie with Posse founder and CEO Debbie Bial, celebrating Posse's 30th anniversary at the Metropolitan Museum of Art, New York, May 22, 2019.

I'm blessed to know Posse's remarkable staff and scholars, and my involvement with them and Posse is the most valuable role of my life. I've been fortunate to do many things in life, including building up Sotheby's and the National Trust, but nothing has come close to giving me the joy and satisfaction I have gained from helping to provide opportunities to thousands of young people. This has been truly important work.

Doing What I Love

23

Raising Funds for Causes

MANY PEOPLE HATE ASKING OTHERS for money. They may find it embarrassing, feel they lack the courage, or believe they don't have the skills to be able to do it well. One of my unusual qualities is that I actually like asking people, companies, or organizations to give money—sometimes huge wads of it—not for myself but for causes that are extremely needy, close to my heart, or both. I don't view it as asking for charity but rather as a way to share my passions. I enjoy giving others the chance to get excited about causes that mean something and to derive the kind of satisfaction that accrues from seeing their philanthropy well spent. It's money that can save lives, build buildings, and enhance the education of children in need. So, for as long as I've been able, philanthropy has always been a large and satisfying part of my life.

A fair bit of judgment is required in going to someone with your hand held out, both in determining whom to ask and for how much. It all comes down to relationships, the knowledge that one has acquired over the years, and a lot of good research on the donor's giving history and potential. If the request is presented properly, I have found that far more people than one would imagine are willing to donate up to the limit of their ability and, almost always, they get pleasure out of doing so.

Over the past four decades I have been involved in raising large sums of money for more than twenty-five projects, mostly involving the welfare of children and institutions relating to the improvement of education. These efforts have been, in my view, some of the most important work I've ever done, and whether it's Posse, Vanderbilt, the Graham School, or so many other causes, I have been rewarded beyond measure by these involvements.

...

DURING MY TIME AT Sotheby's, in 1985, I was asked to help the oldest child welfare agency in America, Graham Windham, which had been founded in New York City in 1806 by Isabella Graham, Sara Hoffman, and Eliza Hamilton, who was the widow of Alexander Hamilton. In the mid-twentieth century, it merged with a similar organization called Windham.

The request centered around the need to restore a campus that existed in Hastings, New York, on the banks of the Hudson River. The campus housed kids from the impoverished inner-city areas of New York who, sadly, could no longer live at home due to abuse, abandonment, or other dire circumstances.

One of the improvements we made was to build two tennis courts for the kids. As I briefly mentioned earlier, we invited Arthur Ashe to come to the campus to give the kids a tennis clinic. Since winning Wimbledon in 1975 with that great tactical victory over Jimmy Connors, Ashe had used his high-profile position in the sporting world to lend his name and time to many projects concerning black youth. With his writings and speeches, he had proved himself to be one of the most intelligent and deep-thinking athletes of his era. And, with his insatiable curiosity, he always liked to test the water. On his arrival at the campus, I remember Arthur asking the kids to put their hands up if they knew who he was. Their faces were blank, and there was no show of hands.

"So, how many of you know who Michael Jordan is?" he asked. Everyone's hand shot up. Arthur laughed, then told them that he was the Michael Jordan of tennis. That got lots of giggles, and he proceeded to have a great clinic for them.

A Graham Windham gala was arranged to celebrate the completion of the $4 million fundraising campaign, but as the date approached, we realized we were almost half a million dollars short of our goal. Suzanne and I put up $150,000 with a Cinderella grant that would expire at midnight. To prevent the grant from evaporating at the midnight hour, guests were asked over dinner to match the $150,000 with $300,000. It worked. We raised the money in time, and hundreds of kids had a decent place to live.

Arthur and Jeanne Ashe with Suzanne and Michael Ainslie
at the Graham Windham gala, April 1986. Photo credit: Arthur Krasinsky.

. . .

I SPENT A LOT of time looking at old buildings during my days with the National Trust and had seen too many pulled down. I always tried to find alternatives to demolition, if possible, and nothing changed when my family and I moved to Palm Beach. Unsurprisingly, it was partly for this reason that I found myself involved with the restoration of the Royal Poinciana Chapel and the adjacent Sea Gull Cottage, which had been the winter home of Henry M. Flagler, a founder of Standard Oil and also the Florida East Coast Railway before he built his much larger main house, Whitehall, in 1905.

In spite of some of the negativism and rigidity of my Southern Baptist upbringing, I consider myself a Christian, believing in a God who loves all people. At the same time that I think that the Catholic Church and many Protestant denominations have largely been corrupted by the men who have controlled them for more than 2,000 years, I also believe that the concept of a church as a gathering place for a community is beneficial for everyone who participates, no matter what his or her belief system. That's another reason I was compelled to take on the project.

The Royal Poinciana Chapel, which sits on a spectacular two-acre site alongside the intercoastal waterway in Palm Beach, was built in 1897 on the grounds of a hotel that Henry Flagler was also building. In 1900, when the original pastor of the chapel died, Dr. George Morgan Ward was approached as a successor. But his reply was abrupt: "I don't want to give cream puff sermons to the idle rich."[1] To his credit, Flagler was not put off by what he called Dr. Ward's "sassy letter" and reached an agreement with the broad-minded pastor. Principles were laid down, the two most important of which were that the church be nondenominational and that it would have the "freest pulpit in America." The Royal Poinciana Chapel still follows those principles, and I have enjoyed being involved. I worked closely with the minister, our dear friend Dr. Bob Norris; chaired the board for a few years; and co-led the fundraising effort to raise $8 million to restore Sea Gull Cottage.

Sea Gull Cottage was built in 1886 by a Denver railroad millionaire named R. R. McCormick who then sold the cottage and adjoining land to Flagler for $75,000.[2] The cottage, which sits with a spectacular view of the intercoastal waterway, had been moved from its original position in Palm Beach and is the town's oldest building. But it was in a bad state of disrepair, and many people on the chapel's board wanted to pull it down, failing to recognize its historic value. I felt differently and, as president of the board, exerted a little influence. I found ready support from fellow board member and former IBM executive Mitchell Watson, as well as Bob Norris, and the three of us set about raising the money.

It took $7.5 million to restore Sea Gull Cottage, but now that people can see the beautiful Queen Anne–style house in all its refurbished glory, I think most agree it was worth it. In the community, we continue to make good use of it as a youth center where, on every Wednesday and Friday night, local kids come to play games and enjoy themselves in a safe environment. It is used for Sunday school and also functions as a music conservatory with frequent piano recitals and other musical events.

However, we weren't quite finished with this historic area of Palm Beach. I was looking for someone who might be interested in having his or her name associated with the beautiful gardens surrounding the Royal Poinciana Chapel, which included one of the city's great landmarks, the 188-year-old kapok tree that stands, majestically, at 150 feet tall.

The opportunity arose when long-time Palm Beach resident and my dear friend Michael Picotte joined me in attending a bluegrass concert at the chapel, listening to the music, looking out over the back lawn toward the kapok tree and the fabulous view onto the intercoastal waterway. As I mentioned earlier, Michael's wife, Margi, is the daughter of the former New York City mayor John Lindsay and was a close friend of Suzanne during their grade school days in New York. We had plenty in common since Michael and Margi have been active donors through their charitable foundation, directed primarily toward improving education.

As we chatted, Michael asked me about the campaign to restore Sea Gull Cottage and create a new fountain in the garden we were viewing. I told him that the only big opportunity we had failed to secure was the naming of the garden we were sitting in. He asked me the required donation, and I said $250,000. The Picottes' home during their early years in Palm Beach had been five blocks away from the chapel, and Michael told me that he often came to the garden with his three kids, bringing them and their family dog to play around the kapok tree. Even though he is a devout Catholic, putting his name to the gardens of an interdenominational church did not seem to worry him. "Let me talk to Margi about this," he said, sounding interested. The concert ended, and a couple of hours later, he called me to say they would do it.

A few months later, we dedicated the Picotte Family Lawn and Kapok Tree with his grown kids and some friends. It was a lovely occasion and, frankly, also the easiest donation of that size that I ever obtained, primarily because I had not even planned to ask my good Catholic friend.

...

A PROJECT THAT HELPED improve educational facilities in Palm Beach came about when our daughter, Serena, went to Palm Beach Day Academy, a school for students from preschool through ninth grade. The head of the school was a remarkable educator named Rebecca van der Bogert, and she and I worked together in developing a vision and master plan for the school. We needed to raise $14 million, which was a lot of money for an establishment that was not even a high school. We knew it was not going to be easy.

For the old Palm Beach families, writing large checks was a way of life. But this was not so with many of the parents at the school, because so many of them had only more recently made their money and had no history of philanthropy. So I knew it would take a bit of educating and explaining about how much benefit could be derived from their generosity. Rebecca and I went to work on them, and eventually, after much arm-twisting, the money started rolling in.

One of the most important improvements we were able to make for the school was the conversion of an old gymnasium into the $5 million

Matthews Cernter for Performing Arts, which features the Matthew and Tracy Smith Family Theater. Seating 350 people, it boasts state-of-the-art lighting, seating, staging, and electronic technology, which provides amazing opportunities for students to perform and for others to learn about producing great plays and other student events. We must have done something right because Bob Nederlander, a good friend and one of the New York theatrical families said, "This is the kind of theater we build!" Since their productions range from *Cats* to *The Lion King* in his company's theaters on Broadway and London's West End, that was quite a compliment to us. The Matthews Center, named for my close friend Will Matthews and his mother who gave the original building, is used for school assembly every morning and has become the heart and soul of the campus.

Another $6 million piece of our campaign was an education building, now known as the Mandel-Palagye Education Center. By the time Rebecca van der Bogert retired in 2016, the benefits of our fundraising project were plain for all to see.

Happily, Suzanne and I are able to be donors as well. This sometimes drives her a bit crazy because she thinks I am an easy touch, being overly generous at times. But, as is the case with the fundraising ventures I become involved with, we focus our giving primarily on educational projects that give kids the chance of a better life. Posse and Vanderbilt University have been at the top of our giving list, what we call our "varsity charities," as well as others, like Graham Windham and the Palm Beach Day Academy.

...

MY FINAL PALM BEACH project started in 2015 when Mort Mandel, a good friend who happened to be ninety-five years old, called me and asked me over for coffee. Mort is a successful industrialist from Cleveland. He and his two brothers built and sold their company, and his recent activities have centered on the Mandel Foundation and its work in the Cleveland area, Palm Beach, and Israel.

In his wonderful folksy way, Mort asked me a big question: "How can I say thank you to the town of Palm Beach? My wife Barbara and I have lived here for fifty-five years and have raised kids and grandkids, and this town has been wonderful to us. We want to do something to show our appreciation." I told Mort I would need to ask the mayor and town council members for their ideas on a good project and come back to him in a few days.

Everyone I talked to had the same response. "We really need a new recreation center," they told me. The one we already had was dated, aging, and at five feet above sea level, it couldn't be renovated. I returned to Mort with this information, and he loved the idea. He quickly stated, "I will put up one-third of the money, up to $5 million, if the town will put up a third, and other citizens will put up a third." The town was easy to convince, but a huge effort was going to be required of me to lead in raising the other third.

I convinced Matt Smith to chair a new 501(c)(3) to be known as Friends of Recreation. I then agreed to be vice chair, treasurer, and chief fundraiser, and we went to work. Matt and his wife Tracy immediately showed their leadership by committing, along with his parents, $750,000 to the recreation-center project.

About halfway through our fundraising efforts, a group of local citizens that we affectionately call the CAVE people (citizens against virtually everything) sued the town to try to stop the project. I was furious, went to tell Mort about this, and let my anger be known. Mort showed me his wisdom that day by calming me down and asking, "Michael, would you rather live in Syria, Russia, or Turkey? Minorities do have their rights. Let's let this play out, and hopefully we will win." Well, Mort was right, and a year later, we did win.

The new Morton and Barbara Mandel Recreation Center ended up costing $13.8 million and was completed in November 2019, when Mort had just turned ninety-eight years old.

Raising the $4.6 million for Friends of Recreation took an enormous effort, since this was not a project on the radar screen of many people. Though education and a lot of arm-twisting were required, we succeeded, with more than 125 families donating between $1,000 and $750,000. While most of the work was satisfying, the bulk of the fundraising fell to me, and it was exhausting. But I had a ball getting to know Mort Mandel, a remarkable man who became a dear friend. And it was also a real joy to be able to have the town name the building the Morton and Barbara Mandel Recreation Center. It is the first building in Palm Beach to be named for a donor who happens to be Jewish. With other recreation facilities in town named Bradley Park, the Phipps Ocean Park, and the Ray Floyd Par Three Golf Course, it was time.

...

I BELIEVE THAT PHILANTHROPY plays an enormous role in the life of the United States and is one of our country's greatest strengths. It enables us to find solutions to social issues in the most creative ways. The Posse Foundation, as I mentioned, is a classic example of a nonprofit that has changed thousands of lives of talented young leaders. It now has a $25 million annual budget; has granted scholarships from our partner universities, totaling $1.4 billion; and enjoys an endowment in excess of $85 million. As I write, there are 3,000 Posse scholars on campuses across America. All the money has been raised through private philanthropy, which is a great tribute to the generosity of those people who responded to our call for help. I take great pride in having played a leading role in building the Posse success story.

I think, as a whole, it's important to remember that we all arrived on this earth with nothing, and we all depart with nothing. It is up to us to share what we are fortunate enough to accumulate in a world that we all know is far from equitable.

24

Connecting People, Creating Beginnings

As anyone who has gotten this far in reading my life story will know, I have been lucky to have done a large number of different things in my seventy-six years. Inevitably, this has required an ability to interact with, get to know, talk to, and listen well to others. I've had the privilege of meeting thousands of folks in every walk of life, from business to government to education to philanthropy. And I believe there's something powerful in the connections we make with people that can create opportunity, bring good out of a situation, and build bridges.

From an early age, I learned the importance of connecting with people as I watched my father interact with them. He engaged with them in a way that demonstrated respect and genuine care. He wanted to help them recognize their potential and be better off in the long run. I don't think I could have had a better mentor.

At some point, I began to see connecting people as a primary role in my life, and now, every day, I try to do something intentional to connect personally with others or connect people with one another. This can involve introducing a Posse scholar to someone who works in a field of interest to the scholar, helping a friend of Serena's find a good summer job, helping a Keegan Fellow get accepted into naval Officer Candidate School, or advising a young professional. Although these involvements may not be viewed as rocket science, they necessitate having the right attitude, being genuinely interested in people, and being accessible and understanding. What are someone's true needs? Who could be useful to them? How might goals be aligned? I think that the more people you know, the easier it is to answer those questions.

You can paint my canvas with a pretty broad brush, from the Washington legislators I dealt with during my time at the National Trust to the many people who sat on the Vanderbilt board with me more than twenty years and all my international contacts in the art world as a result of my time at Sotheby's. There was the USTA board, opening up an entirely new range of friends in tennis and politics like Pam Shriver and David Dinkins, and, from another world, Debbie Bial and The Posse Foundation board and the remarkable Posse scholars. And of course there are the many board members and senior finance executives I met during my fifteen years involved with Lehman Brothers.

Sometimes, connections happened because I was in the right place at the right time or because I was open to them. Other times, I was able to connect with people as a direct result of misadventures I'd had in my life that I was able to work through. In all cases, I'm grateful to have interacted with so many people in different sectors of life, especially since connecting people is something I've always enjoyed.

...

ONE OF THE MORE interesting bridges I was able to help build through personal and professional connections involved Marjorie Scardino, the former CEO of Pearson, once ranked seventeenth on the Forbes list of the World's 100 Most Powerful Women and later a dame of the British empire.[1] Even before all of her considerable successes, she was a little girl who did some rodeo riding while growing up in Texarkana, Texas, and who later grew up to marry one of Lucy Scardino's brothers.

Although Marjorie's varied talents would have ensured a successful life no matter what, it so happened that a series of events involving the breakup of my marriage to Lucy set Marjorie off on a path toward British citizenship. And it had everything to do with the fact that I wanted to get Marjorie's husband, Albert, out of my apartment in New York.

The third Scardino in line, Albert Scardino, met and married this lovely young lawyer named Marjorie Morris. They founded a newspaper in Savannah called *The Georgia Gazette*, which was good at creating head-lines and upsetting local companies with its liberal views, but it wasn't very good at making money. However, before it closed, it took on the local Coca-Cola plant over an issue of radioactive water, and Albert won a Pulitzer Prize for his strong editorials.

At about the same time, Lucy and I ended our marriage, and I took the Sotheby's job in New York, setting myself up as a bachelor with an apartment at 125 East Seventy-Second Street. Not long after I moved in, I got a call from Marjorie, asking me for a favor. She was wondering if I would mind letting Albert have my maid's room at the apartment for a few weeks, since he was joining *The New York Times* and could not afford to rent an apartment of his own.[2] She was planning to continue her legal practice and keep their three children in Savannah for the moment. Albert and Marjorie were family, and of course I said yes.

After Albert moved in, it was fun having him around at the occasional dinner party when, no longer being able to introduce himself as an in-law after Lucy and I divorced, he settled for "outlaw." Our arrangement was fine for a few months, but eventually I found it somewhat restricting on my social life since I started to date young ladies around town. I let Mar-jorie know my feelings about this, and her reply was typical of her. "You need to get me a job in New York. Then, I'll move up there and get Albert out of your hair," she told me. As I mentioned, I like a challenge, so I set about finding Marjorie a job.

I knew exactly to whom I needed to speak. I called my friend Jacques Nordeman, the ubiquitous headhunter. I told Jacques that I needed him to find a job for Marjorie Scardino, the former publisher of a failed newspaper in Georgia. After some laughter and prodding, he reluctantly told me that he was looking for a publisher for the American edition of *The Economist*.

I recalled a dinner I had in London shortly before with Evelyn de Rothschild, the wealthy British aristocrat who was chairman of *The Economist*. I remembered him to be a person with an outrageous sense of humor, the sort of fellow who might be able to take an off-the-wall suggestion in his stride. So I persuaded Jacques to meet with Marjorie and see if he had the courage to put her name forward to Evelyn. I had a feeling Marjorie and Evelyn would hit it off, and they did. Marjorie got the job, and in 1985, she was appointed president of *The Economist*'s North American Division. And, true to her word, she moved Albert out of my apartment.

Suddenly propelled into a position that enabled her to give full vent to her creative talents, Marjorie changed *The Economist*'s image in America through some inventive and sophisticated advertising campaigns. The result was that she tripled the circulation and, after a few years, was promoted to CEO of the Economist Group in London. She, Albert, and their three children moved to London.

In 1997, Marjorie took a big step up when she became CEO of Pearson, which owned the *Financial Times* and 50% of *The Economist*. Marjorie wasted little time in setting that age-old company off on a route to greater focus and profit. Pearson, originally an engineering company formed in Yorkshire in 1844—it built the Blackwall Tunnel in London and the East River Railways Tunnels in New York—under Marjorie's strategic leadership was on its way to becoming the largest educational publishing company in the world. Marjorie began divesting extraneous assets such as Lazard, the investment banking house, and Madame Tussauds, the famous London waxworks.

The acquisition of Simon & Schuster's business and educational division from Viacom pointed the way to a greater emphasis on educational publishing and learning products, as well as moving the company toward digital. By 2011, Marjorie, living up to her British nickname of "Marj in Charge," was overseeing a company with sales approaching £6 billion and profit growing to £942 million.[3] Her impact on the British publishing scene had been recognized long before. In February 2002, a month after Marjorie took British citizenship, the queen made her a dame, the female equivalent of being knighted in the United Kingdom.

Then, after sixteen years in charge of Pearson, she stepped down in 2012 and became the first female member of the board of Twitter. She also joined the board of the MacArthur Foundation and subsequently became its chairwoman. Before leaving Pearson, Marjorie had become the highest-paid female executive of a FTSE 100 company, with a final year bonus of £9.6 million.[4] That was some ride from Texarkana.

It's interesting to think the situation of my divorce from Lucy set off a sequence of events that eventually led to that kind of career trajectory. I happened to be friends with Jacques Nordeman, had previously met Evelyn de Rothschild, and knew of Marjorie's gifts and talents. And, no offense to Albert, but I'm glad I was able to initiate a conversation and spark a connection that ultimately helped bring Marjorie to New York to embark on the next phase of her career. You never know what can happen with your connections. Nurture them well, be observant, start the necessary conversations, and look for ways to help others.

...

MY EXPERIENCE AS A Corning Fellow and later as a member of the board of trustees at Vanderbilt have opened up many connections over the years that have allowed me to invest in the lives of talented student leaders. One of these students was Wyatt Smith, the 2010 Keegan Fellow. Wyatt and I first connected during his four-year term as a YAT, young alumni trustee, on the Vanderbilt Board of Trust. As a YAT, he'd been elected to the position by his senior class and then served on the board as a full voting trustee, contributing significantly to board matters.

Wyatt and I shared a similar set of life experiences. Amazingly, he was from a small town in Alabama, had come to Vanderbilt on a scholarship, was elected president of the SGA, and also won the Keegan to travel the world. Wyatt sat on the Vanderbilt board for four years, and after the Keegan, he spent two years in Birmingham with Teach for America (TFA), starting a program there called Birmingham to Beijing to take inner-city high school students to Beijing for the summer. This program earned him national Teacher of the Year acclaim from TFA. He then entered Harvard Business School, graduating in 2015, and, just as I did, went to work for McKinsey & Company.

He is a wonderful young man, one I am proud to call a close friend, so close that I flew to Lake Placid in 2018 to be part of his and his wonderful bride Meg's wedding festivities. I imagine I'll see him running a big company, a state, or the country one of these days. He's certainly the kind of person who could. Several months after his wedding, Wyatt made the decision to leave McKinsey to become the head of business development for Uber Elevate, an innovative effort to create autonomous flying vehicles to bring commuters downtown from the suburbs. I look forward to following his successes.

...

ANOTHER VANDERBILT STUDENT I'VE had the joy of helping and connecting is Danielle Kitchen, one of the 2018 Keegan Fellows. As the selection board for the fellowship, we immediately took notice of her outstanding academic and leadership record at Vanderbilt and were impressed with the thoughtful and comprehensive nature of the plan of travel she developed, one focused upon the topic of "Identity, Role and Perception of the Military" in some twenty countries across five continents. It was an ambitious plan, and when we interviewed her about it, her fielding of questions about handling risk in difficult environments was impactful; she demonstrated great poise, strong verbal communication skills, and an amazing entrepreneurial spirit in her response. We awarded her one of the fellowships.

In planning and executing her research, she reached out to Condoleezza

Rice. Knowing Danielle's focus and goals, several members of our selection committee suggested she also meet with senior level military and diplomatic contacts. She quickly and professionally followed up with each of them, further building her network of contacts. One of these contacts produced a two-hour meeting and ongoing regular communication with Gary Luck, a US Army four-star general. He then introduced her to retired general Ann Dunwoody, the first female four-star general in the military. It was fascinating to watch Danielle build relationships with various military and diplomatic leaders, and we were impressed with her ability to take initiative and further build on those connections.

In May 2018, Danielle departed on her Keegan travels. She started in France, where she met with the US senior military official in the country. After speaking with former US ambassador Craig Stapleton, she diverged from her original plans and instead attended the Tocqueville Foundation conference on democracy in the West. Other conference attendees included Dan Coats, US director of national intelligence, and Hubert Védrine, former minister of foreign affairs of France. A couple of months later, Danielle was invited by the US ambassador to NATO, Kay Bailey Hutchison, to attend the NATO Summit in Brussels under the auspices of the Atlantic Council and their Millennium Fellows program.

From these and other connections, she proceeded to meet throughout Europe with US defense attachés and other senior military leaders, both American and indigenous. In four short months, Danielle had traveled to France, Iraq, Brussels, the Netherlands, Sweden, the United Kingdom, Ukraine, Jordan, Lebanon, and Israel and was preparing to go to Afghanistan. Not only was she learning through this travel, but she was also interviewing fifteen to twenty-five civilians and military officials in each country, as well as learning from host families and Vanderbilt friends.

She has written extensively on each country and synthesized her observations. She's also shown an incredible ability to gain people's trust and obtain nuanced views on the delicate questions of the role of the military in some intensely difficult political environments. "In my year traveling,"

Danielle says, "I learned to become more resourceful and ingenious than was possible inside a classroom. I met people around the world with incredible strength and resilience who had faced great adversity and, against all odds, maintained faith in humanity. I also saw tragedy and poverty worse than anything I could've imagined, the kind that makes your heart break time and time again."[5]

She left for her fellowship having deferred a consulting offer, a common post-Vanderbilt path. But after the experiences and conversations of the Keegan, she says, "I realized how lucky I was—and we were—as Americans for our country and the opportunities here. I felt as though I owed that back through service, so I sent back my corporate signing bonus and applied to the US Navy." Because of Danielle's significant accomplishments, the perspective she'd gained in traveling the world, and her resolve to serve her country, she was selected for a position with the US Navy. "My friends may have been confused at the change of heart, but I knew Michael and the fellowship board would not be. The fellowship changed me and my trajectory in many ways, and I'll be thankful for it and for everyone I met along the journey forever," she says.

I'm thrilled to have been able to play a role in connecting Danielle with some of the opportunities she's had. She's a self-starter and a natural leader, and I believe she has what it takes to make a major contribution to our military and our country.

...

BEING ABLE TO HELP Debbie Bial and Vanderbilt University in a way that launched The Posse Foundation and led to so many genuinely exciting and fulfilling relationships with the kids is one of the things that has given me the most pleasure. I have been happy to answer the call in helping a great number of Posse scholars over the years. Monique Nelson is one of those. She was a member of Posse 3 at Vanderbilt, and her success in the field of advertising has been astounding. Monique is the CEO and the primary owner of the multicultural advertising agency UWG, formerly known as UniWorld, which was founded by Byron Lewis Sr. in 1969.

I had been able to connect Monique with Peter Georgescu,[6] the inspirational former CEO of Young & Rubicam, when she told me she was thinking of buying UniWorld. "Peter is an advertising god," Monique told me. "He couldn't have been more helpful and gracious with his time and advice. Being in the advertising world, he knew about my partners and talked me through the pitfalls of purchasing a business."

Monique has now moved the UWG headquarters to Brooklyn, New York, which makes her feel very much at home because that was where she was born. The company is thriving under her leadership and has a host of top clients, including Ford, Lincoln, Home Depot, and the Marine Corps. She continues to emphasize the need for multicultural companies to be accepted on an equal footing in the advertising world and is particularly proud of the Culture Labs, which UWG set up. The program recruits from local New York colleges, and the students involved feed their own ideas and projects into the mix as they prepare themselves for a possible career in marketing after graduating.

"We hope some of them will return to work for us, just as a few Posse scholars have," says Monique, who has never forgotten the unexpected opportunity she was given at such an early age to attend Vanderbilt. For her, it is all about collaboration and the support you get from your "posse" no matter where you are, as well as, of course, the need to make the right connections. She once told someone, "I never had to worry about that, because Michael was there for me. He always comes up with the best of the best, and you never have to worry about the caliber of person he connects you with."[7]

● ● ●

RYAN LETADA IS ANOTHER Posse scholar I was able to help as he realized his ambitions. Now in his early thirties, Ryan has made the need to raise the profile and respect of the Filipino diaspora worldwide his life's work. Seizing on the opportunities offered by the digital age, Ryan has created a for-profit organization called Next Day Better, which aims to connect the 11 million Filipinos around the world through digital story-telling. More broadly, his goal is to "rebrand migration," showing all the enormous societal benefits of free movement of people throughout the world. His clients include Mailchimp, AARP, Doctors Without Borders, and others. I introduced Ryan to Austin Fragomen, the founder of the largest law firm specializing in immigration, now with sixty-five offices across the globe. Austin has joined me and Monique Nelson and others on Ryan's advisory board and is now a client of Next Day Better.

Ryan tells others that he was lucky enough to win the Ainslie Alumni Achievement Award in 2014 and has been trying to do it justice. "I see it as a responsibility, something that will last through a lifetime as I try to bring people together and open up opportunities for Filipinos wherever they are. Obviously, I needed funding to get this project started, and Michael was always there for me, a continuous presence in my life, helping me to fulfill my potential. He has always been so generous with his introduc-tions. He's been a facilitator and a guide. He is amazing," he once shared.[8]

Ryan is starting to zero in on specific projects that can have an imme-diate impact on the health of people in the Philippines. To that end, Next Day Better has teamed up with Doctors Without Borders so that it can bring pressure on Pfizer to reduce the cost of its pneumonia vaccine (the drug company is the leading manufacturer of the vaccine). When Ryan started the campaign with Doctors Without Borders, Pfizer was charging forty-five dollars a shot, which is far too expensive for most people in the Philippines. The aim was to get it reduced to five dollars. Pfizer was bring-ing in nearly $6 billion a year from that vaccine alone.[9]

With the right partners, Ryan believes his media impact company, which creates a storytelling platform for diaspora communities, can make a difference. But he recognizes that people who look like him don't always get invited onto the big stage to have their message heard. Ryan knows he needs to innovate and develop world-changing ideas to accomplish his goals. He tells people, "Everyone needs help, especially someone like me because I am the first entrepreneur in my family. So, it is vital that I have people like Michael as a role model and draw on his support. He took a chance and invested in me. I am so grateful."

. . .

IN AUGUST 2000, I had just finished a friendly golf match at the Round Hill Club in Greenwich, Connecticut, with the great golf photographer and my good friend Jules Alexander. He mentioned to me that he was going to "do a book on Tiger Woods" and hoped to find someone to partner with him on the project. I knew that, once again, I was in the right place at the right time. I'd always found Jules's work to be extraordinary, I loved golf, and I enjoyed connecting with people on new experiences. Without hesitation, I extended my hand and told him, "You just found your partner."

Jules traveled to more than fifty golf tournaments, positioned himself perfectly on each course, and, with great patience and an expert eye, waited to capture the essence of who Tiger Woods is, not only as a powerful athlete but also as a human being with real humor, ambition, drive, and grace. For *Tiger Woods in Black & White* (available on Amazon), we worked with professional golfer Johnny Miller to bring together many of the great golf journalists of our time. Jim Nantz, the CBS Sports commentator; Dave Anderson, columnist for *The New York Times*; Damon Hack, a senior writer for *Sports Illustrated*; James Dodson, author of *Ben Hogan: An American Life*; and Lorne Rubenstein, author of *A Season in Dornoch,* all contributed essays to this book. The result was a collection of stunning photos and commentary that told the bigger story of arguably the greatest golfer of all time.

. . .

I ENJOY BEING ABLE to connect people in a way that inspires others, makes people think, and offers greater perspective. And I'm always glad to have opportunities to meet more people and build relationships. Inevitably, these names and faces come to mind at later points in life. You never know when one person's story might need to intersect with another, and simply in connecting the two, you open a door.

Moving Forward

25

Living a Good Life

A NOSE FOR TROUBLE BEGAN AS a way of telling my kids, my grandkids, and my many Posse scholar friends about my life. I want them to know my journey, my tough patches, and how I overcame them, and I want them to know my victories and how I achieved them. Much of my working life occurred thirty or forty years ago. Even my own children know little about those periods of my life. So, here it is.

Hopefully it can educate, provoke some questions and discussions about how to face challenges, and maybe even inspire. I have had a blessed life. With great parents, wonderful friends and mentors, and an incredible life partner and children, countless opportunities have been presented to me. Along the way, I have encountered my share of adversity. But then again, everyone faces lots of adversity. The big question is, how does one deal with adversity? A good life is one that overcomes it, learns from it, and tries not to repeat the mistakes. Gaining that understanding is my wish for my readers.

Acknowledgments

I **AM INDEBTED TO MANY OLD** and new friends who helped make my book a reality.

First is my daughter Serena, and her friends Sofie and Sara, and others who sat up many late nights listening to my stories and hearing me read drafts. They always wanted to hear more. It made me think my ancient history might have some relevance to their generation.

My longtime confidant, Joni Evans, the publishing guru, kept encouraging me along the way, often as I went quiet for months at a time.

Many an hour was spent with my friend and cowriter Richard Evans. His encyclopedic knowledge of the history of tennis, the royal family, and the art world, coupled with his ability to use his phenomenal journalistic education to research people and events and then to elaborate on my recollections, all made for a richer book.

Owen Williams, the outstanding South African tennis professional and sports executive, is a wonderful friend and mentor who also led me to Richard Evans. Richard helped Owen write his rich life story, *Ahead of the Game*.

Mary Simses, my dear friend and a talented author in her own right, gave much advice on writing and website development and applied her photographic skills when called upon.

I am indebted to Jessica Choi, my editor from Greenleaf Book Group. She was outstanding in giving flow to the book, in asking what I learned from each experience, and generally helping me link together many disparate experiences.

My copy editor, Lisa Norton, was a wonderful part of my team and helped get my technological skills somewhat improved.

Understanding and explaining the intricacies of the Lehman bankruptcy was made much easier by frequent consultation with my friend Tom Russo, the General Counsel of Lehman Brothers Holdings and subsequently, AIG.

And finally, my wife Suzanne was a constant booster, feeling my story was important to tell.

Notes

CHAPTER 1

1. Thomas A. Russo, "Too Big to Fail: Perspectives on Systemic Risk & the Lehman Bankruptcy," *The Journal on the Law of Investment & Risk Management Products: Futures & Derivatives Law Report 38, no. 8* (September 2018): 4.

2. Ibid., 5.

3. Patrick Fitzgerald, "J. P. Morgan to Pay $1.42 Billion to Settle Most Lehman Claims," *The Wall Street Journal*, January 25, 2016; Lehman Brothers Holdings Inc. and The Official Committee of Unsecured Creditors of Lehman Brothers Holdings Inc. v. JPMorgan Chase Bank, N.A., No. 11-cv-6760-RJS, United States District Court, Southern District of New York (September 30, 2015), at 5.

4. Jonathan Stempel, "JPMorgan to pay $1.42 billion cash to settle most Lehman claims," *Reuters*, January 25, 2016.

5. Stephen Labaton and Edmund L. Andrews, "In Rescue to Stabilize Lending, U.S. Takes Over Mortgage Finance Titans," *The New York Times*, September 7, 2008, https://www.nytimes.com/2008/09/08/business/08fannie.html; Kimberly Amadeo, "What Was the Fannie Mae and Freddie Mac Bailout?" *The Balance*, updated June 29, 2019, https://www.thebalance.com/what-was-the-fannie-mae-and-freddie-mac-bailout-3305658.

6. Matthew Karnitschnig, Deborah Solomon, Liam Pleven, and Jon E. Hilsenrath, "U.S. to Take Over AIG in $85 Billion Bailout; Central Banks Inject Cash as Credit Dries Up," *The Wall Street Journal*, September 16, 2008, https://www.wsj.com/articles/SB122156561931242905.

CHAPTER 2

1. George Ainslie was also an expert on butterflies as this excerpt, which appeared in the *Florida Entomologist* of June 1922, attests. It is a long and detailed work, which could be entitled, "The Birth of a Butterfly," but here is a short description of a larva emerging from its shell: "After breakfasting on the egg-shell, the small larva selects a location on

the upper surface of the leaf, near the edge and begins to construct its retreat by placing a layer of silk fibers on the surface. The effect of this is quickly seen in the gradual curling of the blade. . . . The skill with which the weak and apparently helpless larva manipulates the thick, stiff corn leaf is remarkable."

2. In 1913, John H. Patterson fired Thomas Watson, one of the young executives at NCR. Perhaps Patterson had been offended by the precocious Watson interrupting a meeting a few years earlier to say, "We don't get paid for working with our feet—we get paid for working with our heads." Watson then scrawled the word "THINK" on the blackboard. THINK became the slogan and trademark of the company Watson would go on to create: IBM. "International Business Machines," *Fortune*, January 1, 1940, http://fortune.com/1940/01/01/international-business-machines/.

CHAPTER 9

1. Office of the Comptroller of the Currency, "Historic Tax Credits," Community Developments: Fact Sheet, July 2017, https://www.occ.gov/topics/community-affairs/publications/fact-sheets/pub-fact-sheet-historic-tax-credits-jul-2017.pdf.

2. Main Street America, "Reinvestment on the Rise," https://www.mainstreet.org/mainstreetimpact.

CHAPTER 10

1. I want to note that the restructuring of the agreement was painful and difficult for the Rockefeller family, as David said to me on more than one occasion during my years at Sotheby's: "Why did we not get our agreement cast in stone before you departed the National Trust?" Many thanks to the Rockefeller brothers for sharing their family legacy with the public.

2. Sarah Booth Conroy, "Orchids and Orientalia," *The Washington Post*, March 8, 1981, https://www.washingtonpost.com/archive/lifestyle/1981/03/08/orchids-and-orientalia/7f91c09b-33a1-4fdb-b51d-54cb74a1e718/?utm_term=.781620b0fdc8.

3. Guy Hawtin, "How St. Bart's Lost Its Landmark Case," *New York Post*, February 26, 1986.

4. Like all the Scardinos, Lucy is incredibly bright and equally complicated. As a young woman, she went off to college at Sacred Heart in Purchase, New York. She did not graduate but chose to marry Tom Oxnard, the heir to a sugar fortune from Savannah, Georgia. They quickly had three daughters. Divorce followed a few years later, and Lucy settled back in Savannah in the coach barn behind her parents' beautiful historic home on Gaston Street.

   Lucy was the eldest of seven siblings. Their father, Dr. Peter Scardino, a brilliant urologist and surgeon, was known in the family as Scar Daddy. He moved the family to Savannah after finishing residency training in urology at Johns Hopkins in Baltimore. His eldest son, Peter, followed in his footsteps as a urologist and became chief of surgery at Memorial Sloan Kettering Cancer Center (MSKCC) in New York. Peter is one of the leading cancer urologists in the country. As well, he is known for his brilliant bedside manner. He knows how to speak truthfully but with sensitivity to patients. On top of it all, he is incredibly bright and talented at selecting other really good doctors. This is why he had a great run as the top surgeon at MSKCC. He stepped down as chief of surgery after ten years in that role. I consider Peter among my closest friends, and happily, I have been able to remain close to virtually the whole Scardino family.

CHAPTER 11

1. Alfred Taubman was the son of Jewish parents who fled Poland before World War II to settle in Michigan. He grew up in Detroit and studied architecture, although he never graduated from the University of Michigan. He soon turned his design skills toward building shopping malls—vast, luxurious shopping malls, the likes of which America had never seen. His Short Hills Mall in New Jersey, built in 1980, rapidly became one of the largest grossing malls in the country, and Taubman was well on the way to making his fortune. The personal satisfaction must have been immense because his father had been wiped out financially by the Great Depression. Al had been forced to start earning money at the age of nine. When, in 1983, with money to spare, he began looking for acquisitions and Sotheby's came under pressure from a hostile takeover effort by Cogan and Swid and their General Felt Industries (a New Jersey carpet manufacturer), he stepped in and saved Sotheby's.

2. Peter Osnos, "The Yanks Are Coming," *The Washington Post*, May 3, 1983, https://www.washingtonpost.com/archive/lifestyle/1983/05/03/the-yanks-are-coming/2c56ec72-297e-48f1-b5cd-f38bac8cd9a1/?utm_term=.e5e690db3500.

3. A. Alfred Taubman, *Threshold Resistance: The Extraordinary Career of a Luxury Retailing Pioneer* (New York: HarperCollins, 2007).

CHAPTER 12

1. David Gelles, "Obituary: Saul Steinberg, Corporate Raider," *Financial Times*, December 10, 2012, https://www.ft.com/content/7bd9b95c-42ff-11e2-aa8f-00144feabdc0.

CHAPTER 13

1. "Update Regarding Sotheby's Buyer's Premium," Sotheby's, www.sothebys.com/en/articles/sothebys-buyers-premium-update

2. Sotheby's, "Sotheby's Announces Definitive Agreement to be Acquired by Patrick Drahi," PR Newswire, June 17, 2019.

CHAPTER 14

1. Leslie Wexner believed in owning competing brands and wanted Sotheby's to start a separate auction house under the Parke-Bernet name, but despite numerous attempts, he found no support from his fellow board members.

2. Max Fisher was the oldest member of the Forbes 400 when he passed away at the age of ninety-six in 2005.

3. Christopher Mason, *The Art of the Steal: Inside the Sotheby's-Christie's Auction House Scandal* (New York: G. P. Putnam's Sons, 2004).

CHAPTER 15

1. Ralph Blumenthal and Carol Vogel, "Chief Witness Accuses Former Boss at Sotheby's," *The New York Times*, November 20, 2001.

2. Suzanne Muchnic, "Van Gogh Painting Sells at Record $82.5 Million: Art: 'Portrait of Dr. Gachet' Is Auctioned to a Japanese Gallery. The Previous High Was $53.9 Million," *Los Angeles Times*, May 16, 1990, https://www.latimes.com/archives/la-xpm-1990-05-16-mn-262-story.html.

3. Rita Reif, "A $27 Million Loan by Sotheby's Helped Alan Bond to Buy 'Irises,'" *The New York Times*, October 18, 1989.

4. Calla Wahlquist, "Alan Bond: The Rise, Spectacular Fall and Rise Again of the America's Cup Hero," *The Guardian*, June 5, 2015, https://www.theguardian.com/sport/2015/jun/05/alan-bond-the-rise-spectacular-fall-and-rise-again-of-the-americas-cup-hero.

5. Carol Vogel and Ralph Blumenthal, "The Autonomy of Sotheby's Chief Is Scrutinized in Antitrust Case," *The New York Times*, November 30, 2001.

6. Carol Vogel, "Auction House Indictments Focus on the U.S. Executive," *The New York Times*, May 4, 2001, https://www.nytimes.com/2001/05/04/business/auction-house-indictments-focus-on-the-us-executive.html.

CHAPTER 16

1. Gene Scott was also one of the most remarkable athletes Yale has ever known. He earned sixteen varsity letters for tennis, soccer, lacrosse, and ice hockey, and there was seemingly no sporting discipline at which he could not excel. After practicing for a few hours on the tennis court, Gene would trot over to the athletic field at Yale and promptly outjump the high jumpers who had been toiling all afternoon. Following an amazing career in professional tennis, he continued to play racket sports at a high level into his fifties.

    When Gene started suffering blackouts in his late sixties, no doctor in New York could find the cause. It was only when a friend finally took him to the Mayo Clinic that he was diagnosed with a rare heart condition for which there was no cure. Gene was in the Mayo Clinic's coffee shop soon after he had been told the news when he collapsed and died at the age of sixty-eight.

    The extent to which he was missed became clear when a memorial service on Fifth Avenue overflowed onto the street. His lovely wife, Polly, and his two young children bore the ordeal stoically, and Suzanne and I were there to mourn the premature loss of a dear friend. Polly remains a dear friend and has recently married Jim Maher, expanding on her prodigious tennis abilities to share his passion for skiing.

    Even today, people in the tennis community will be heard asking, "I wonder what Gene would have thought?" when some big issue arises. He was called the conscience of the game and with good reason.

2. "Serena Williams Wins 18th Slam," ESPN.com, September 8, 2014, http://www.espn.com/tennis/usopen14/story/_/id/11484243/2014-us-open-serena-williams-beats-caroline-wozniacki-win-3rd-straight.

3. "Serena Williams Wins Windy Open," ESPN.com, September 8, 2013, http://www.espn.com/tennis/usopen13/story/_/id/9652185/2013-us-open-serena-williams-wins-17th-grand-slam-title; Associated Press, "Rafael Nadal Wins 13th Slam Title,"

ESPN.com, September 9, 2013, http://www.espn.com/tennis/usopen13/story/_/
id/9656100/2013-us-open-rafael-nadal-bests-novak-djokovic-title-caps-stellar-13.

4. I was later able to convince David Dinkins to join the board of The Posse Foundation,
where he has served with great distinction, attending most board meetings, and always
found ways to inspire Posse scholars.

5. David Dinkins's action led to a battle between him and his mayoral successor, Rudy
Giuliani, who tried to get the agreement torn up. Giuliani, more interested in the votes
of Queens' residents living near the Tennis Center, was livid when Dinkins refused and
signed a longer standing agreement with the USTA. As a result, Giuliani boycotted the
opening ceremony of the Arthur Ashe Stadium in August 1997. Allowing his personal
dislike of Dinkins to interfere with a function honoring a man of Ashe's stature and
reputation was, to my mind, a poor political decision.

CHAPTER 17

1. Patricia Cohen, "Lehman Brothers, a Family Saga, as Viewed by Some Who Lived It," *The
New York Times*, April 17, 2019, https://www.nytimes.com/2019/04/17/business/lehman-
brothers-theater.html?smid=nytcore-ios-share.

2. "The Economic Outlook: Chairman Ben S. Bernanke Before the Joint Economic
Committee, U.S. Congress," Board of Governors of the Federal Reserve System, March
28, 2007, https://www.federalreserve.gov/newsevents/testimony/bernanke20070328a.htm.

3. Andrew Ross Sorkin, *Too Big to Fail: The Inside Story of How Wall Street and Washington
Fought to Save the Financial System—and Themselves* (New York: Penguin Books, 2010).

4. Todd Purdum, "Henry Paulson's Longest Night," *Vanity Fair*, Hive, October 2009.

5. Andrew Clark, "How Close Are Goldman Sachs's Connections with the US Treasury?"
The Guardian, August 10, 2009, https://www.theguardian.com/business/andrew-clark-on-
america/2009/aug/10/goldman-sachs-aig-treasury (January 2019).

6. Laurence M. Ball, "The Fed and Lehman Brothers" (paper prepared for a meeting of the
NBER Monetary Economics Program, July 14, 2016).

7. Russo, "Too Big to Fail," 6.

8. Joshua Zumbrun, "What AIG Really Owes Taxpayers," *Forbes*, September 1, 2009,
https://www.forbes.com/2009/09/01/aig-bailouts-fed-business-washington-aig.
html#4c3b84ef70f8.

9. Mary Williams Walsh, "A.I.G. Lists Banks It Paid with U.S. Bailout Funds," *The New York
Times*, March 15, 2009, https://www.nytimes.com/2009/03/16/business/16rescue.html.

10. Clark, "How Close."

11. Jon Shazar, "Hank Paulson Killed Lehman Brothers 'Cause Karma's A
Bitch," Dealbreaker, September 11, 2018, https://dealbreaker.com/2018/09/
hank-paulson-killed-lehman-brothers-cause-karmas-a-bitch.

12. Russo, "Too Big to Fail," 2–3.

13. Laurence M. Ball, "Ten Years On, the Fed's Failings on Lehman Brothers Are All Too Clear,"
The Guardian, September 3, 2018, https://www.theguardian.com/commentisfree/2018/
sep/03/federal-reserve-lehman-brothers-collapse.

14. Ibid.

15. Peter Eavis, "Fed Fretted Over Reaction to Demise of Lehman," *The New York Times*, February 21, 2014.

16. Ibid.

17. Thomas A. Russo, "Too Big to Fail: Perspectives on Systemic Risk & the Evolving Regulatory Landscape" (presentation to New York University Law and Management of Financial Services Businesses, September 2016).

18. Phil Angelides, Bill Thomas, et al., *The Financial Crisis Inquiry Report: Final Report of the National Commission on the Causes of the Financial and Economic Crisis in the United States* (Washington: United States of America Financial Crisis Inquiry Commission, 2010).

19. Jim Puzzanghera, "Ex-Lehman CEO Blames Government for Firm's Collapse," *Los Angeles Times*, September 2, 2010, https://www.latimes.com/archives/la-xpm-2010-sep-02-la-fi-crisis-inquiry-20100902-story.html; Dan Wilchins, "Lehman Files for Bankruptcy, Plans to Sell Units," *Reuters*, September 14, 2008, https://www.reuters.com/article/us-lehman/lehman-files-for-bankruptcy-plans-to-sell-units-idUSN09279 96520080915.

20. Tamora Vidaillet and Veronique Tison, "Letting Lehman Go Was a Big Mistake," Patrick Graham, ed., *Reuters,* https://www.reuters.com/article/us-france-economy/letting-lehman-go-was-big-mistake-french-finmin-idUSTRE49735Z20081008 (accessed January 2019).

21. My YPO forum became so close that we still meet regularly, some thirty years after our founding. A key to our forum's dynamics is the fact that we have five female CEOs in our group. It makes our meetings much more fun and valued, since we get female perspectives that are often even more insightful than those of our male colleagues. My forum includes Joni Evans, Josie Natori, Kay Koplovitz, Anne Fuchs, Karen Pearse, Massimo Ferragamo, Jon Linen, John Greeniaus, Peter Price, Ken Walker, Bruce Nobles, and John Castle.

CHAPTER 18

1. Oonagh McDonald, *Lehman Brothers: A Crisis of Value* (Manchester, UK: Manchester University Press, 2015).

2. Andrew Ross Sorkin, *Too Big to Fail: The Inside Story of How Wall Street and Washington Fought to Save the Financial System—and Themselves* (New York: Penguin Books, 2010).

3. Ibid.

4. David Reilley, "Closing the Repo 105 Loophole," *The Wall Street Journal*, March 26, 2010, https://www.wsj.com/articles/SB10001424052748704896104575139813742667200 (accessed April 2019).

5. Anton R. Valukas, *Report of Anton R. Valukas*, Examiner (Chicago: Jenner & Block, 2010), https://online.wsj.com/public/resources/documents/LehmanVol1.pdf.

6. Lehman Brothers Holdings Inc. and The Official Committee of Unsecured Creditors of Lehman Brothers Holdings Inc. v. JPMorgan Chase Bank, N.A., No. 11-cv-6760-RJS, United States District Court, Southern District of New York (September 30, 2015), at 5.

7. Laurence M. Ball, "The Fed and Lehman Brothers" (paper prepared for a meeting of the NBER Monetary Economics Program, July 14, 2016).

CHAPTER 19

1. Hugh Hildesley was also an excellent auctioneer. In 1994, after sixteen years as an Episcopal rector, he would return to Sotheby's as vice chairman and a business winner, while continuing his occasional pastoral activities of both marrying and occasionally burying Sotheby's friends and family. He would also later christen our daughter, Serena Hooker Ainslie, in 1998 shortly after her birth. Hugh and his wife, Connie, have remained dear friends.

2. We have traveled the world with Serena's dear friend Sofie Tabernilla and Sofie's parents, Armando and Holly, and their son Christian. Over the past decade we have been with them to Morocco, Croatia, Bali, Cambodia, Laos, and Thailand, with a most recent trip to Tanzania, Uganda, and Dubai.

3. Suzanne is a woman of remarkable depth. Some years back, she set out on a project that entailed a detailed study of all the world's religions—Christianity, Judaism, Kabbalah, Hinduism, Sikhism, Islam, Taoism, and the nontheistic religion or philosophy called Buddhism, among numerous others. It was a quest that obviously required a huge amount of study, and Suzanne immersed herself in videos and books while searching for an answer to the basic question of "Why are we here?"

Her upbringing had been one of rigid Catholicism, but early in her life, she rejected the fundamental tenets of the Catholic Church. Whatever disciplines the church was attempting to lay down for its young flock obviously were not working, because Suzanne, along with several of her classmates, used to enjoy taking out the rubber bands that were used to hold their braces in place and flick them through the grill of the confessional at the poor priest. At a young age, she refused to accept the bizarre Catholic concept that she was going to hell if she died on the way to confessionals.

Years later, even her nephew Alexander Mejia and his bride-to-be, Justine Wardrop, recognized Suzanne's spiritual side by asking her to perform their wedding in the fall of 2017. After getting over the shock and then finding an easy way online to become an ordained minister, she presided over what many called "the most personal and moving wedding they could recall."

4. Ironically, Suzanne is a distant cousin of Blanchette Hooker Rockefeller, both of them direct descendants of Thomas Hooker, the founder of the Colony of Connecticut, now known as Hartford, Connecticut.

CHAPTER 22

1. Debbie Bial, in an interview with Richard Evans, August 2017.

2. "Posse Facts & Figures," Posse Foundation, https://www.possefoundation.org/posse-facts.

3. To see a full list of the partner universities, please visit https://www.possefoundation.org/supporting-scholars/college-university-partners.

4. This quote and the following from Jamaal from Jamaal Nelson, in an interview with Richard Evans, July 2017.

CHAPTER 23

1. "History of the Royal Poinciana Chapel," Royal Poinciana Chapel, https://royalpoincianachapel.org/about/history/.

2. "Buildings & Grounds," Royal Poinciana Chapel, https://royalpoincianachapel.org/about/buildings-and-grounds/.

CHAPTER 24

1. "The 100 Most Powerful Women: #17 Marjorie Scardino," *Forbes*, August 30, 2007, https://www.forbes.com/lists/2007/11/biz-07women_Marjorie-Scardino_MCY3.html.

2. The apartment at 125 East 72nd Street was a hard sell. Our dear friend Ritchey Goodwin was only able to close a sale to good friends by offering their six-year-old daughter a color TV if she told her parents how much she loved it. And it worked.

3. Dugald Baird and Dan Sabbagh, "Pearson Chief Executive Marjorie Scardino to Step Down," *The Guardian*, October 3, 2012, https://www.theguardian.com/media/2012/oct/03/pearson-marjorie-scardino-step-down.

4. Ibid.

5. This quote and the following from Danielle Kitchen, in an interview with Richard Evans, June 2017.

6. Peter Georgescu has an inspirational life story. He was left behind in Romania as a child for five years, between the ages of eight and thirteen, because the Iron Curtain fell when his parents were visiting the United States, and they could not return. His father would have been killed had they done so. Tragic confirmation of that came when Peter's grandfather was arrested as a political threat and murdered in prison. At the age of nine, Peter and his brother were sent to a work camp. Romanian diplomats in New York approached Georgescu's parents and suggested their children would be sent to them if they were prepared to spy for the Communist government. Bravely, the Georgescus refused and went public, causing a huge furor in the press. Their cause was taken up by President Eisenhower, and the children were ultimately released. Despite arriving with little education and speaking not a word of English at the age of thirteen, Peter was granted entry to Exeter Academy and proved himself such a quick learner that he went on to Princeton and Stanford and ended up as a trainee at Young & Rubicam Inc. in 1963. Among numerous other achievements as he rose through the ranks, Georgescu ensured that the company created the largest database on global branding. He wrote an important op-ed piece for the *New York Times* called "Capitalists, Arise: We Need to Deal with Income Inequality", served as the chairman and CEO of Young and Rubicam from 1994 to 2000, and went on to become the chairman emeritus of the company.

7. Monique Nelson, in an interview with Richard Evans, June 2017.

8. Ryan Letada, in an interview with Richard Evans, June 2017.

9. Emily Mullin, "Pfizer Posts Positive Data for 20-Strain Pneumococcal Vaccine," BioPharma Dive, April 16, 2019, https://www.biopharmadive.com/news/pfizer-posts-positive-data-for-20-strain-pneumococcal-vaccine/552846/.

Index

About the Authors

MICHAEL AINSLIE has been a champion of education for decades. His passion has been The Posse Foundation, which he helped launch in 1994. Michael was Posse's first board chair, serving for thirteen years and continues on the Posse board.

Posse finds young leaders from public and parochial high schools in ten major cities and sends them to one of Posse's fifty-seven elite university partners as a cohort of ten Posse scholars. They receive a full-merit leadership scholarship. More than 9,200 Posse scholars have won $1.4 billion in scholarships, and they are graduating at a rate of 90%. Posse's goal is to have these young people assume leadership positions in the workforce, and they are doing just that. Posse alums are now partners in law firms, one is president of a college, another is CEO and owner of an advertising firm, another started a charter school, and many are teaching at the university and high school levels.

Michael had a distinguished business career serving as president and CEO of Sotheby's from 1984 to 1994, leading a transformation of the worldwide auction business. Previously he was president and CEO of the

National Trust for Historic Preservation from 1980 to 1984. While at the National Trust, he helped rewrite the tax law to provide a 25% investment tax credit for investment in historic buildings. This incentive radically changed the landscape of historic preservation.

Michael is a graduate of Vanderbilt University and Harvard Business School, and he studied abroad as a Corning Foundation World Travel Fellow. He is a trustee emeritus of Vanderbilt University and has served on the boards of the United States Tennis Association, the St. Joe Company, and Lehman Brothers.

He and his family reside in Palm Beach, Florida.

RICHARD EVANS, born in Paris, has been in journalism for sixty years, mostly writing about tennis—and commentating on Wimbledon for BBC Radio—but also as a foreign correspondent for the London Evening News in New York in the 1960s. He was on Robert Kennedy's campaign in 1968 and reported from Vietnam.

Evans has written or edited more than twenty books, including his own story, *The Roving Eye: A Reporter's Love Affair with Paris, Politics & Sports*.